Major is Harmonic
(and Other Essays)

Randy Vincent

Cover Graphics and Book Design - Attila Nagy

©2024 Sher Music Co., P.O. Box 445, Petaluma, CA 94953
www.shermusic.com
No part of this book may be reproduced
in any form without written permission from the publisher.
All Rights Reserved. International Copyright Secured
ISBN - 978-1-883217-10-5

TABLE OF CONTENTS

Introduction: The "Loneliest" and "Forgotten" Scale 1

Chapter 1 : Defending the Harmonic Major 5

Chapter 2 : Some Basic Applications 15

Chapter 3 : "Hidden Chords" and the Relationship to "Bebop" Scales 23

Chapter 4 : Some Practice Suggestions 29

Chapter 5 : Some Thoughts About Bebop Scales 39

Chapter 6 : A Different Approach to Improvising Using Cells 49

Appendix A : Harmonic Major Scale Revisited 63

Appendix B : Bebop Scales Revisited 70

Appendix C : Cellular Improvisation Revisited 77

Appendix D : Some Interesting Ways to Think About Scales 91

INTRODUCTION
THE "LONELIEST" AND "FORGOTTEN" SCALE

This book was inspired by Dan Greenblatt's great work *Minor is Major!* and thus the unusual title. Greenblatt contends that minor scale theory (harmonic minor more specifically) gets relatively neglected when compared to major scale theory, and his book does a great job at correcting the situation.

Pervasiveness of melodic scales over harmonic ones
My contention is that the harmonic scales (both major and minor) are relatively neglected when compared to the "melodic" scales (the major and the melodic minor). Greenblatt seems to agree when he states in his Introduction: "Interestingly, the melodic minor scale has not been 'underprivileged' in the way that the harmonic minor has. The characteristics and uses of the MM (melodic minor) scale have been analyzed at length by a number of prominent writers." Rick Beato in his YouTube on the harmonic major scale calls it the "loneliest" and the "forgotten" scale. Most contemporary Jazz Improvisation methods don't even give it a mention.

It strikes me as possible that the augmented 2nd in the "harmonic" scales contributes to their neglect, while the major and melodic minor scales and their modes have only major and minor seconds, making them easier to hear and sing and play.

Some thoughts about the terminology of "major," "minor," "melodic," and "harmonic"
Dan Greenblatt has an interesting take on the terms "major" and "minor" in his Introduction and I won't rehash it here, but my understanding in music theory is that "major" means "large" and "minor" means "small." So we have large versions ("major") of the intervals of 2nds, 3rds, 6ths, and 7ths, and also smaller versions ("minor") of those intervals.

The major scale and the melodic minor scale (and their modes) are the only two possible seven-note scales that contain only major and minor 2nds with no augmented 2nds and with no consecutive minor 2nds. Why is this important? Because when you stack 3rds from the scale they will always be major or minor 3rds and so will produce the tertian (harmony built from 3rds) triads and seventh chords, etc. that we use in our harmonic system. So we can see that these scales can be viewed as collections of not just pitches, but of chords. This is shown in the example on the following page.

Major and Melodic Minor scales shown as collections of Tertian chords

Cmajor scale diatonic 3rds:

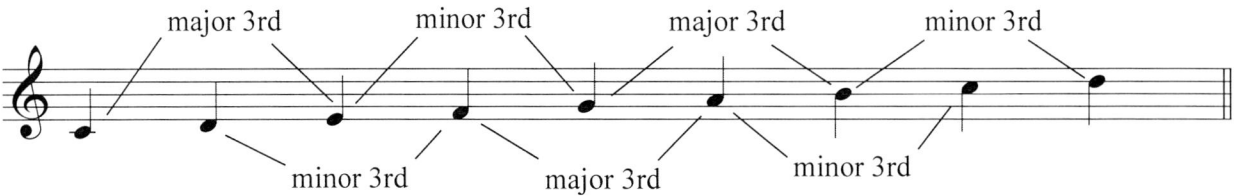

C major scale diatonic 7th chords:

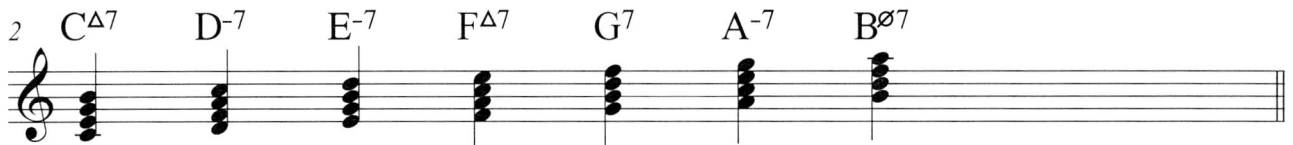

C melodic minor scale diatonic 3rds:

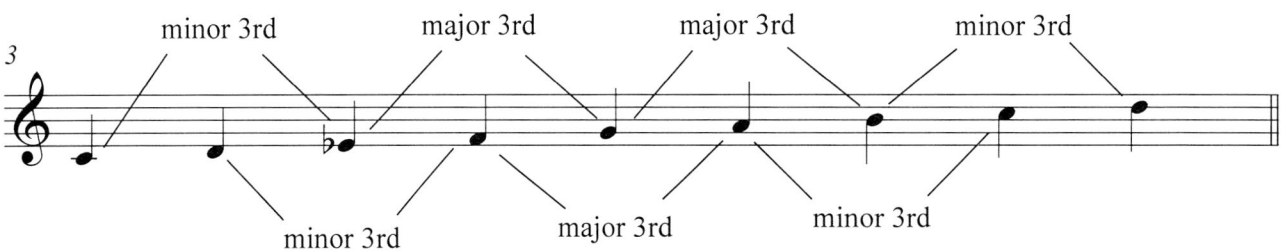

C melodic minor scale diatonic 7th chords:

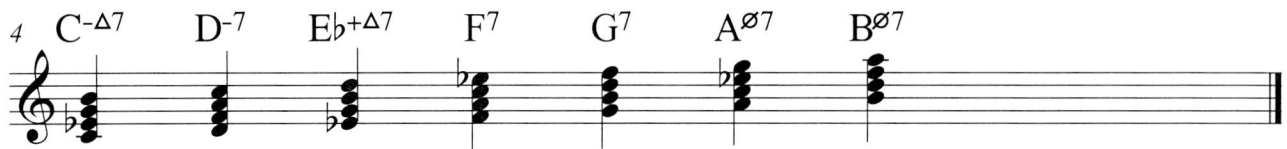

CHAPTER 1: *DEFENDING THE HARMONIC MAJOR*

Only two other seven-note scales can be seen as collections of the tertian (harmony built from 3rds) chords, and those are the harmonic minor and the harmonic major scales (and their modes). They each have one augmented 2nd but all their diatonic 3rds are major or minor. The major and melodic minor scales give us $^\triangle 7$, -7, 7, $^\varnothing 7$, -$^\triangle 7$, and $^\triangle 7\sharp 5$ chords, but the diminished 7th chord is absent until we introduce the harmonic scales. This has resulted in most contemporary Jazz methods relying on eight-note symmetrical diminished scales to cover the diminished 7th chords, but our study of the harmonic scales reveals some more "lyrical" ways to melodize these diminished 7th chords. These harmonic scales are shown on the following page in the key of C (C harmonic major and C harmonic minor) with their augmented 2nds (A♭ to B♮ in both cases) and their full diminished 7th chords (B°7 in both cases).

Greenblatt has covered the harmonic minor brilliantly in great detail, so I won't rehash that except as may occasionally prove necessary to clarify a point about the harmonic major.

The layout will include chapter 1, defending the use of the harmonic major scale, including examples from actual recorded solos and melodies and chord voicings by great jazz musicians. Next will be chapter 2, examining how to apply the harmonic major scale to actual playing situations. Then chapter 3 will look at "hidden" chords in harmonic major, and the relationship to the so-called "bebop scales." Chapter 4 has suggestions about how and what to practice.

Additional thoughts about bebop scales and cellular improvisation
Next will be supplemental information. Chapter 5 will delve into some thoughts and observations concerning the bebop scales, and chapter 6 will present a different way to think about how to develop cellular improvisational vocabulary.

Appendices
Finally there will be four appendices that will revisit the topics with lots of music examples to practice and introduce some hopefully new thoughts that you might find useful (or at least interesting).

Harmonic Major and Harmonic Minor scales shown as collections of Tertian chords

C harmonic major scale:

C harmonic major scale diatonic 3rds:

C harmonic major scale diatonic 7th chords:

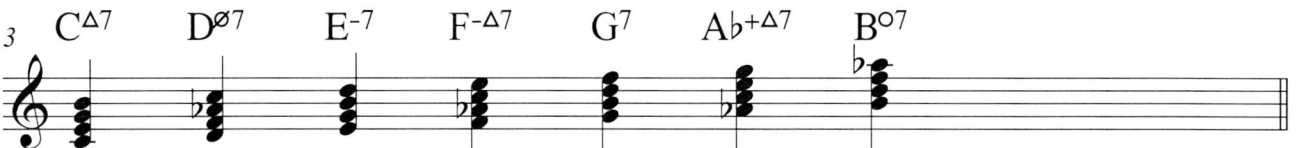

C harmonic minor scale:

C harmonic minor scale diatonic 3rds:

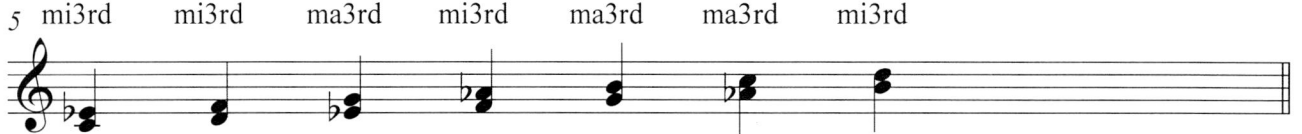

C harmonic minor scale diatonic 7th chords:

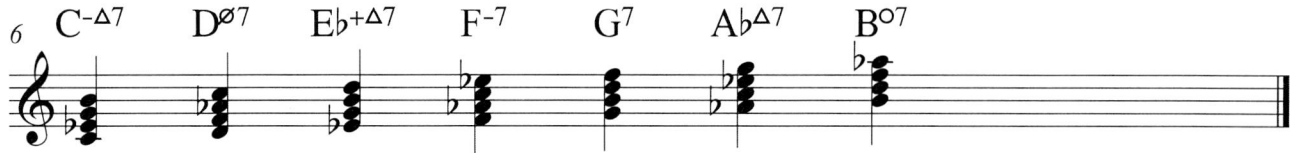

CHAPTER 1
DEFENDING THE HARMONIC MAJOR

Harmonic Major (Major scale with flat six) and its harmonies
The easiest way for me to think of the harmonic major scale is to see it as a major scale with a flatted sixth step, but another way to look at it is to see it as a harmonic minor scale with a major third. In the key of C this would be the notes C, D, E, F, G, A♭, and B. The 3rds would be major from C, minor from D, minor from E, minor from F, major from G, major from A♭, and minor from B (see Ex.1.1).

Ex.1.1

C harmonic major diatonic thirds

The diatonic triads are C major, D diminished, E minor, F minor, G major, A♭ augmented, and B diminished.

Ex.1.2

C harmonic major diatonic triads

The diatonic 7th chords are C△7, Dø7, E-7, F-△7, G7, Ab△7#5, and B°7 (see Ex.1.3).

Ex.1.3

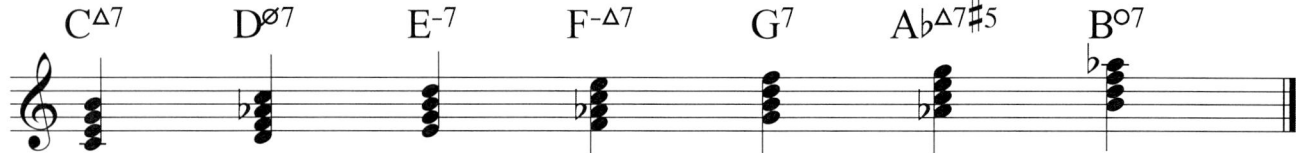

The interesting thing to do next is to look at what the diatonic extensions would be, so C△7 has a ♮9 (good), a ♮11 (not good), and a ♭13 (not so likely unless it's voiced as a #5 with the natural 5 raised up above as if it were an extension, which actually happens sometimes). See Ex.1.4 first measure.

Ex.1.4

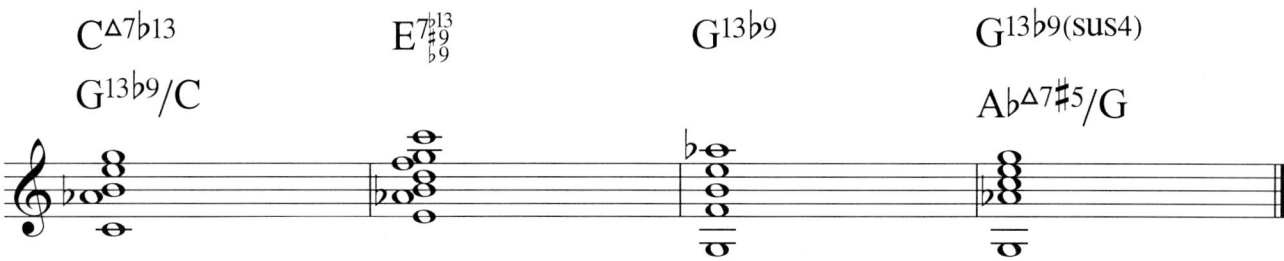

This could also be called Eadd#9/C. The Dø7 has a ♮9 (good), a ♮11 (also good), ♮13 (unusual but certainly not bad). The E-7 has a ♭9 (not so good), a ♭11 (what? Sounds like a major 3rd!), and a ♭13 (we'll see). The F-△7 has a ♮9 (good), a #11 (exotic), and a ♮13 (good). The G7 has a ♭9 (good), a ♮11 (can be OK when used as a 7sus♭9 chord. See Ex.1.4 fourth measure), and a ♮13 (very good, giving that classic 13♭9 sound). The Abmaj7#5 has a #9 (exotic), a #11 (good), and a ♮13 (can be tricky with the #5). The B°7 has a ♭9 (not so good), a ♮11 (good), and a ♭13 (good).

Thinking about these extensions (both the usable and the ones to avoid) suggests some interesting points. One point is the fairly common occurrence of Dø7 going to G7♭9 (especially G13♭9) and resolving to C△7 can be seen as a harmonic major cadence. Some examples include "What Is This Thing Called Love," "Night and Day," "I Love You," and "All of You" (it seems that Cole Porter was quite fond of this sound). The F-△7 (and its partner F-6 suggested by the ♮13) going back to C major is your classic sub-dominant minor cadence.

CHAPTER 1: *DEFENDING THE HARMONIC MAJOR*

Of particular interest is the ♭11 on the E-7 sounding like a major 3rd. The A♭ sounds like G♯. (See Ex.1.4 second measure.) Treating it as a 3rd now makes the chord into an E7 with a ♭9 (now very good), a ♯9 (also very good), and a ♭13 (also now very good). It is now the same as an "Altered" dominant scale but with a ♮5th and avoiding the ♭5th that Greenblatt sometimes found to be objectionable (*Minor is Major!* page 44 and 45). It also has both the ♭9 and ♯9. Big fun.

Some actual examples of Harmonic Major usage

OK, first, a disclaimer. I do not know if any of the players featured in the examples that follow were thinking of using (or naming) the harmonic major scale, or what their sources of inspiration were, but the examples demonstrate that the notes and harmonies of the harmonic major scale really do occur in the actual recorded history of jazz.

Ex. 1.5 is a line from the Wes Montgomery tune "SOS" that descends in step-wise motion all the way through the A♭ harmonic major scale.

Ex. 1.5

Ex. 1.6 is from a Freddie Hubbard solo where he plays all of the F harmonic major scale over a C13♭9 chord.

Ex. 1.6

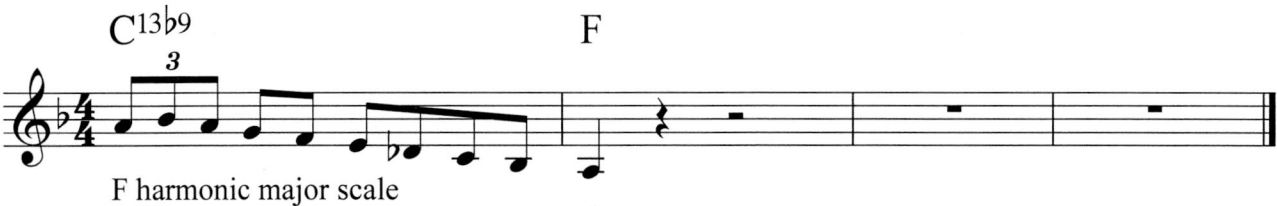

Ex. 1.7 is from a Tom Harrell solo that is a subset of the F harmonic major scale. Only the C note is absent, demonstrating that not every note from the complete scale needs to be used every time.

Ex. 1.7

from a Tom Harrell solo:

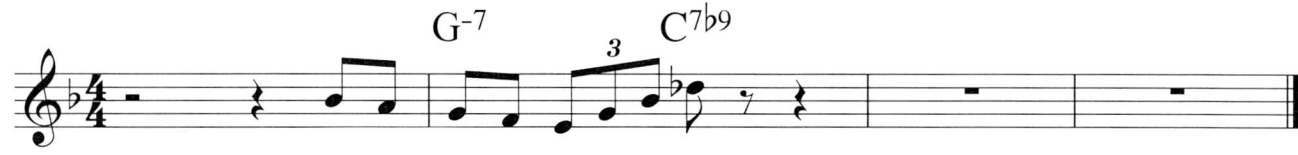

F harmonic major scale

Ex. 1.8 shows Tom Harrell using the entire F harmonic major scale before resolving back into a subset of the regular F major scale.

Ex. 1.8

from a Tom Harrell solo:

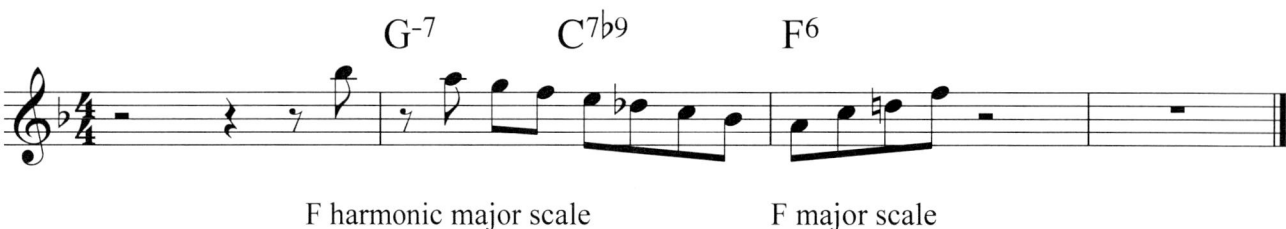

F harmonic major scale   F major scale

Ex. 1.9 is from a Charlie Parker solo where he uses a sequence employing the B♭ harmonic minor scale and the A♭ harmonic major scale to create a classic bebop turnaround.

Ex. 1.9

from a Charlie Parker solo:

B♭ harmonic minor scale   A♭ harmonic major scale
   with chromatic passing tone   with chromatic passing tone

CHAPTER 1: *DEFENDING THE HARMONIC MAJOR*

Ex. 1.10 shows Charlie Parker using all of the notes from the B♭ harmonic major scale on F7♭9 in a ii-V-I in B♭ major.

Ex. 1.10

from a Charlie Parker solo:

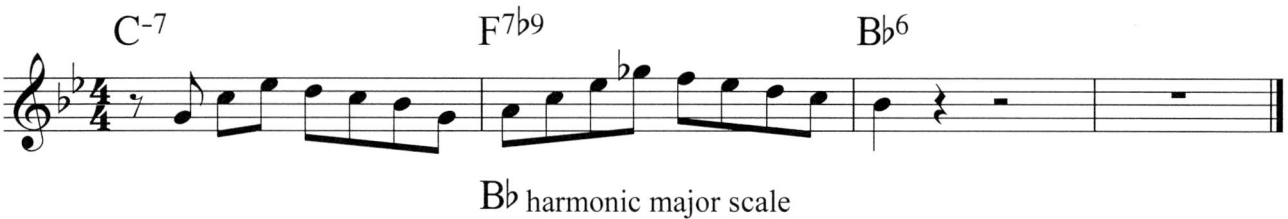

B♭ harmonic major scale

Ex. 1.11 is a famous ii-V-I from a well known Charlie Parker tune, Donna Lee.

Ex. 1.11

from Donna Lee: Charlie Parker

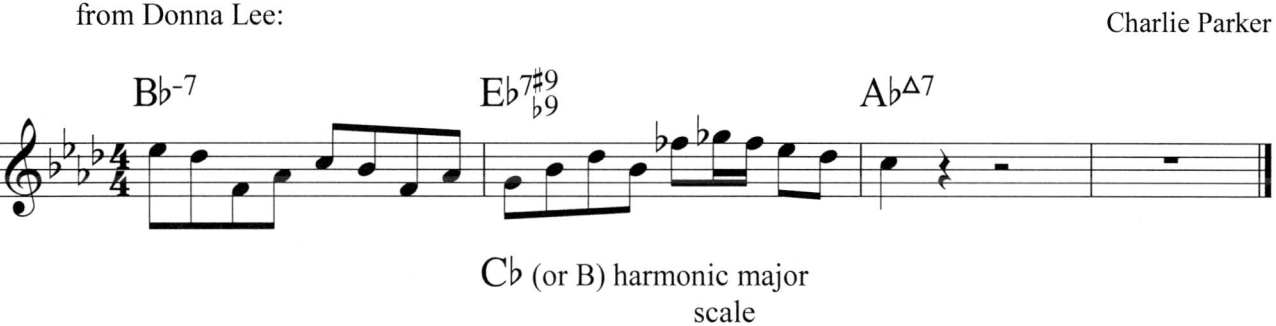

C♭ (or B) harmonic major scale

The ♭9 and ♯9 combination on the V chord might seem to imply an E♭ Altered dominant scale, but notice the B♭, which is the ♮5th. So the line is a subset of C♭ harmonic major (remember that the III chord in harmonic major is a dominant with ♭9 and ♯9 and ♭13 but with a ♮5th), but is also a subset of E♭ half-whole diminished scale. If you really hate C♭, re-write that measure using all sharps and think in B harmonic major.

Ex. 1.12 is a line from Joe Pass that uses a subset of the G harmonic major scale on the D13♭9 chord. The usual scale taught for D13♭9 is the D half-whole diminished scale, but notice that Joe isn't doing that because his line includes the G♮.

Ex. 1.12

from a Joe Pass solo:

G harmonic major scale

Ex. 1.13 is another line from Joe Pass using the same subset used in 1.8, but over A^{ø}7 as well (from the third note on).

Ex. 1.13

from a Joe Pass solo:

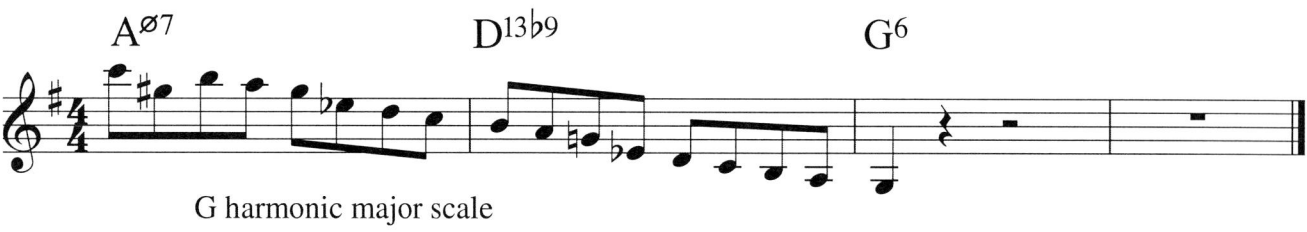

G harmonic major scale

Ex. 1.14 shows a ii-V-I in C major from Joe Pass with the G7 treated as a III chord borrowed from the E♭ harmonic major scale.

Ex. 1.14

E♭ harmonic major scale

CHAPTER 1: *DEFENDING THE HARMONIC MAJOR*

Ex. 1.15 shows the last four bars (before the solos) of Herbie Hancock's great jazz classic "Dolphin Dance."

Ex. 1.15

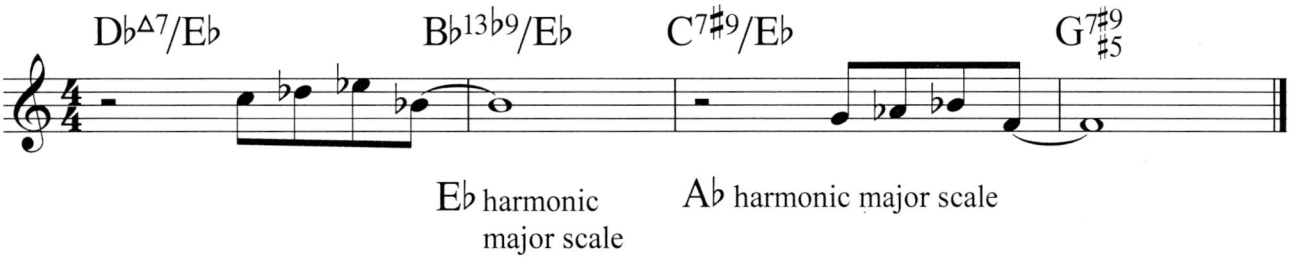

from Dolphin Dance: Herbie Hancock

The voicing that Hancock played for the Bb13b9/Eb resembles an Eb△7#5 with a ♮5 (the melody note) voiced up on top. This makes the #5 more accurately called a b13, resulting in the Eb harmonic major scale analysis. The usual choice of Eb half-whole diminished for Bb13b9 doesn't work well here because the Eb bass note is the ♮4th of Bb. The typical choice of the Altered scale for the C7#9/E is also contra-indicated by the G♮ in the melody, making the Ab harmonic major scale a better choice.

Ex. 1.16 shows a voicing from the tune "When All Is Said and Done" by the great jazz pianist and composer Billy Childs.

Ex. 1.16

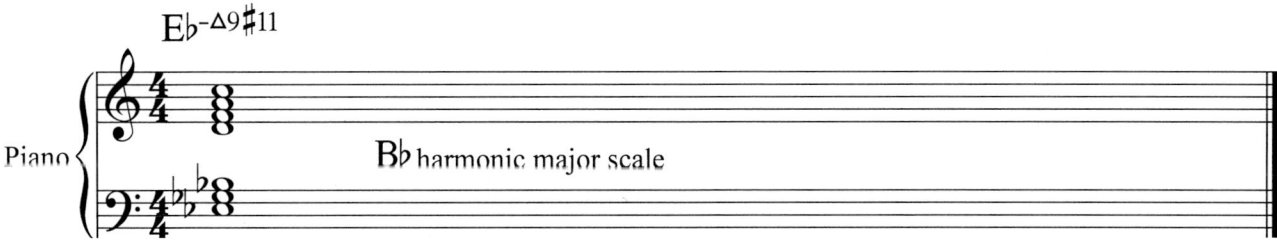

from When All Is Said and Done: Billy Childs

The chord symbol says Eb-9△7#11, which can be seen as a D minor triad voiced over an Eb minor triad. I've included the melody note, C, on top of the voicing. This results in a seven-note scale spread out in 3rds, and is definitely the Bb major harmonic scale.

There are many other examples to be found, but I think that is enough to get the point across for now.

MY PERSONAL HISTORY WITH HARMONIC MAJOR

Very early in my attempts at jazz improvisation I worked with a saxophone player who gave me an original 1953 copy of *The Lydian Chromatic Concept of Tonal Organization* by George Russell. It may have been the earliest attempt at a theoretical method for jazz improvisation as far as I know. Russell had three main seven-note scales that were stacked in such a way as to show the vertical implication of the chords derived from the scales and the variations that result from the slight variations in the scales. The first scale was Lydian (which, being the fourth mode of the major scale, contains the same chords as the major, but revealed in a different order), the second was Lydian Augmented (the third mode of melodic minor), and the third was called "Lydian Diminished," which is Lydian (with a ♯4) but with a minor 3rd (the fourth mode of harmonic major, as it turns out). Russell had his own quirky way of naming the chords found in his scales and I quickly found it more useful for my own thinking to convert them to names that seemed more conventional, so I soon started thinking of the Lydian Augmented as a mode of melodic minor (just one note different from major, the ♭3), and the Lydian Diminished as a mode of major with a ♭6 (again just one note different from major). Up until that time I had just learned and practiced the major scale and the harmonic minor. This was well before the glut of jazz methods that became available later.

Being a guitar player I was naturally on the lookout for helpful jazz guitar books. One that I found very useful was *Joe Pass Guitar Style* by Joe Pass and Bill Thrasher. In the middle of page 13 was an example with the chords A⌀9 to D13♭9 to G△7, using C ascending melodic minor on the A⌀9. The following text says "The F♮ in this last example could be played as F♯, to sound like the major 3rd of D7 and the major 7th of G." That results in the G harmonic major scale. On page 21 in the text under the first three examples we find: "Line 3 uses the B♭ major scale, but the G is flatted to conform to the chord sound. The F7 chord might be played as F13♭9." That's the B♭ major harmonic scale all the way. I recognized right away the equivalence to Russell's E♭ Lydian Diminished.

Around this same time I started studying from *A Modern Method For Guitar* by William G. Leavitt in three volumes. It had these occasional theory pages on how to select chord scale relationships for improvisation. It was based on a concept that I think of as following a "path of least resistance" through the changes and developing the scale knowledge to deal with each chord in context rather than the "cookie cutter" approach of "one size fits all" (such as if you see a mi7, play dorian). Using Leavitt's approach I found many places where harmonic major was either the best choice or at least as good a choice as anything else, even though he never taught that scale in his method, and I could only find one brief mention. It's in Vol. III on page 122 where he says for "ALT 9 on V7, II7, I7 use Real Melodic Minor from ♭7 of chord … or Major scale with ♭6 … from intended tonic."

Following Leavitt's methodology the answer to what to do with an E7 popping up in the key of C major is to sharp the G note. All the others are already in the key of C and the result is an A harmonic minor scale. But what if we interpret the G♯ as an A♭? Now keeping the other notes from the key we have C harmonic major. I began to get great results thinking this way, especially on the secondary dominants of the minor diatonic chords (V of ii, V of iii, and V of vi). This lead to discovering new ways of dealing with diminished 7 chords that can be analyzed as secondary dominants as well. So, for example, if we are playing "Witchcraft" in F, the second chord (A♭°7) can take C harmonic major. The same is true for the A♭°7 that is the second chord in "Corcovado." This helped me to feel much happier with my playing.

CHAPTER 1: *DEFENDING THE HARMONIC MAJOR*

A few years later I encountered *Jazz Guitar Single Note Soloing Vol.1* by Ted Greene. On page 94 he begins his presentation of "Altered Dominant Scales" (not to be confused with what is now usually called the Altered Dominant Scale, the seventh mode of melodic minor). He presents three types, Type 1, which is the V chord in harmonic major, Type 2, which is the V chord in harmonic minor, and Type 3, which is the III chord in harmonic major. Greene dislikes thinking in parent scales and prefers thinking from the root of the chord, but I was able to recognize that two of his altered dominant scales (Type 1 and Type3) were actually modes of harmonic major, the fifth mode for Type 1 and the third mode for Type 3. On page 72 of Vol.2 Greene introduces four types of what he calls "mi7b5 scales." The one that he identifies as Type 4 is basically a dorian mode with a ♭5, which turns out to be the second mode of harmonic major.

At the end of 1980 I moved from Cocoa Beach, Florida to Petaluma, California and began teaching and playing in the San Francisco Bay Area. Several of my students were also either students or former students of the legendary guitarist Dave Creamer, and they showed me pages of lines that he had written out for them to practice. Some of the pages were exclusively ii-V-I lines utilizing what Creamer called the "major flat six" scale. By the way, that is the name I was still using at the time. It was some years later that I found out that it had its own "official" name (harmonic major).

About this same time I was working with saxophone master Mel Martin and encountered a tune of his that upon first listening seemed to have the common progression Ami to A-△7 to A-7 to A-6. Mel's chart had these chord names: Ami to A♭△7♯5 to C/G to F♯°7. His melody had a prominent G natural note on the A♭△7♯5 which would obviously clash with A-△7. Once again the expected G♯ note is really A♭, resulting in C harmonic major as the best scale choice for the situation.

Some years later I found out that jazz fusion guitar master Allan Holdsworth was teaching about what he called his "ten most useful scales." To briefly summarize, the first four scales in his system are equivalent to our major, melodic minor, harmonic minor, and harmonic major scales. Holdsworth was basically self-taught and used his own way of naming and conceptualizing the scales. His scale no.1 he calls minor and is the same as dorian, therefore a mode of the major scale. His scale no.2 he calls minor-major 7 and is the same as melodic minor. His scale no.3 he calls minor-major 7 with a flat 6 and is the same as harmonic minor. His scale no.4 he calls minor-major 7 with a raised 4 and is the same as George Russell's Lydian Diminished scale, the fourth mode of harmonic major.

Since I had learned the major scale first and had developed a grasp of how it could be found in any key and in any register throughout the range of my instrument it made sense to me to relate everything else to it in the most simple way possible. So I see the melodic minor as a major scale with a ♭3, the harmonic major as a major scale with a ♭6, and the harmonic minor as the relative major scale with a ♯5, although it is also easy for me to see it as a sort of "hybrid" of the other two, that is, a major scale with both the ♭3 and the ♭6.

Perhaps the deepest theoretical presentation I've seen was in the amazing book *Harmonic Experience* by W. A. Mathieu, although it doesn't deal with jazz applications but rather focuses on use for serious composition. Mathieu looks at scales from the perspective of what he calls the "Magic Mode." It is a theoretical source for seven-note scales that all have a perfect fifth, but the 2nd can be major or minor, the 3rd can be major or minor, the 4th can be perfect or augmented, the 6th can be major or minor, and the 7th can be major or minor. In chapter 26 in example 26.14 we find what I have been calling the C harmonic major scale. Mathieu calls it "Harmonic Minor over Major," basing the name on the fact that the upper tetrachord is identical to the harmonic minor while the lower tetrachord is major. Example 26.22 shows a scale that Mathieu calls "Major over Gypsy Minor," again named from the tetrachords (Gypsy Minor is what I learned as a youth as Hungarian Minor, basically harmonic minor with a ♯4), so the upper tetrachord is major while the lower tetrachord has a minor 3rd and an augmented 4th, making it identical to George Russell's Lydian Diminished scale, the fourth mode of harmonic major. At the beginning of the chapter Mathieu shows a mode that he doesn't name but calls an "unfamiliar but attractive mode." It has a ♭2nd and a ♭7th and is the fifth mode of harmonic major, the same as Ted Greene's Altered Dominant Type 1. These modes are the ones that are members of Mathieu's Magic Mode and the harmonic major scale.

One other source I came across later was from bebop era guitarist Joe Puma. His book *Extended Scale Playing For Guitar* didn't appear until the 1990s but his playing and recording career goes back well into the 1950s. Puma's scale system also has our four scales, including major, melodic minor, harmonic minor, and one that he calls a "mi7♭5 scale." It is basically a dorian mode with a flat 5. It turns out to be the second mode of harmonic major, which we saw as Ted Greene's mi7♭5 scale Type 4. On page 37 Puma suggests that the Dmi7♭5 scale can be applied to not only D°7, but to G13♭9 and to E7♯5♭9♯9 as well. The scale has the ♮5 of E so the ♯5 is more accurately a ♭13. The G13♭9 corresponds to Greene's Altered Dominant Type 1 and the E7♭9♯9♭13 corresponds to Greene's Altered Dominant Type 3.

Of course we now have the Internet so you can find many other informative sources. I would suggest starting with Rick Beato's YouTube presentations on the major harmonic scale and then go from there. You'll find that it is not totally neglected and forgotten, just a little underrated.

CHAPTER 2
SOME BASIC APPLICATIONS

Some "Micro Etudes" Based on Changes From Standard Tunes
Now let's try some examples that demonstrate some of the possible applications of the harmonic major scale for improvisation on chord changes taken from various standard tunes from the usual jazz repertoire. I am calling them "micro etudes" because they are short "snapshots" rather than complete choruses or even complete sections. They more or less resemble the type of lines that may happen during an improvised solo, although I have constructed them specifically to demonstrate the harmonic major scales in pure form without any added chromatics so you can hear the scales over the chords more clearly.

Ex. 2.1 shows a line based on the chord changes from the first seven bars of the tune "Witchcraft."

Ex. 2.1

Early in my career I played either diminished arpeggios or the whole-half diminished scale whenever I saw a diminished chord, but I was rarely happy with the result. Perhaps because my first exposure to the major harmonic scale was its fourth mode, called the Lydian Diminished Scale in George Russell's *Lydian Chromatic Concept,* my early application was on diminished chords. The first two bars are F major bebop with some chromatic passing tones, followed by the C harmonic major scale applied to the A♭ diminished chord. The C7♯9♭13 chord shows a line that is an incomplete A♭ harmonic major scale. The G♮ note is omitted, resulting in a six-note (hexatonic) scale that could be analyzed as a subset of the C Altered scale (7th mode of D♭ melodic minor) with the G♭ omitted. This hexatonic scale is thoroughly covered in my book *Line Games.* Looking at it as A♭ harmonic major rather than as D♭ melodic minor eliminates the worry mentioned by Dan Greenblatt in *Minor is Major!* about using the more "out" sounding G♭ note.

Concerning the choice of C harmonic major for the A♭ diminished chord, my thought process is based on William Leavitt's method that I think of as "following the path of least resistance." The key is F major, and the A♭ diminished chord has only two notes that are not diatonic to that key, the root A♭ and a B♮. The B♮ puts us temporarily in the key of C major while the A♭ makes it a C harmonic major scale.

Ex. 2.2 shows a line based on the chord changes from the first seven bars of the tune "Corcovado."

Ex. 2.2

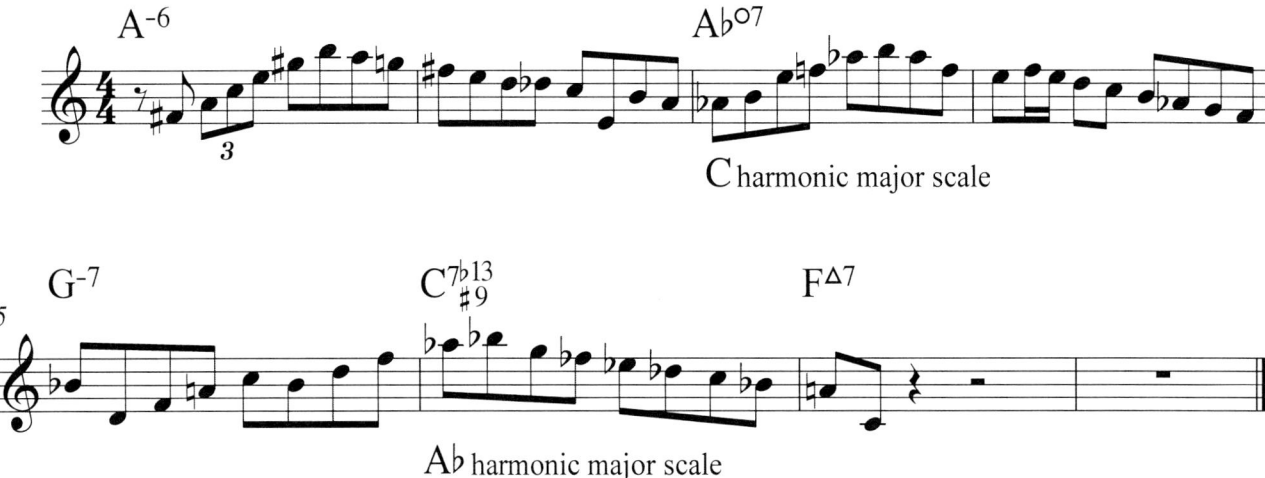

The harmonic major applications are the same as in the last example, but the A♭ harmonic major scale uses all seven of its notes this time. The first six notes on the A-6 is an extended arpeggio from the A melodic minor scale, while the rest of the A-6 is treated as if it were D9, using typical D dominant bebop scale vocabulary.

Ex. 2.3 shows a line based on the chord changes from bars three, four, and five of the great standard ballad "Body and Soul."

Ex. 2.3

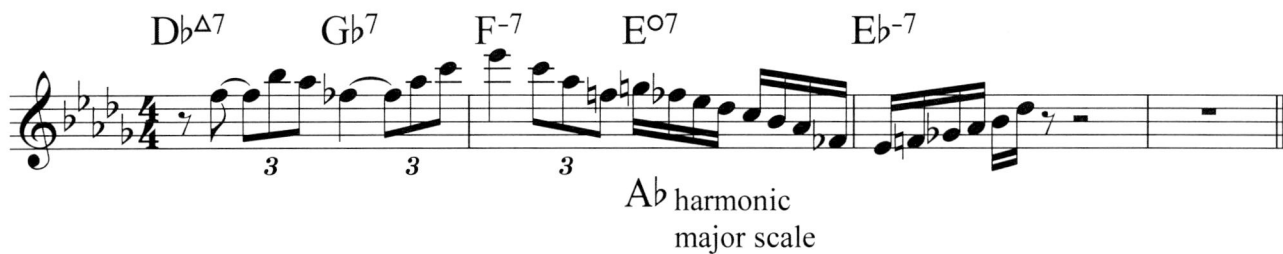

CHAPTER 2 : SOME BASIC APPLICATIONS

The E°7 chord is really an F♭ diminished, a diminished chord on the ♭3 of the key going to the ii chord, the same as the diminished chords in the last two examples. The related scale is A♭ harmonic major. From these examples we can extract a "rule," that when a diminished chord occurs on the ♭3 of a major key (or on the I, or the ♯IV = ♭V, or on the vi) the harmonic major scale on the fifth of the key can be used.

Ex. 2.4 shows a progression that is so common to so many tunes that I won't bother with a name.

Ex. 2.4

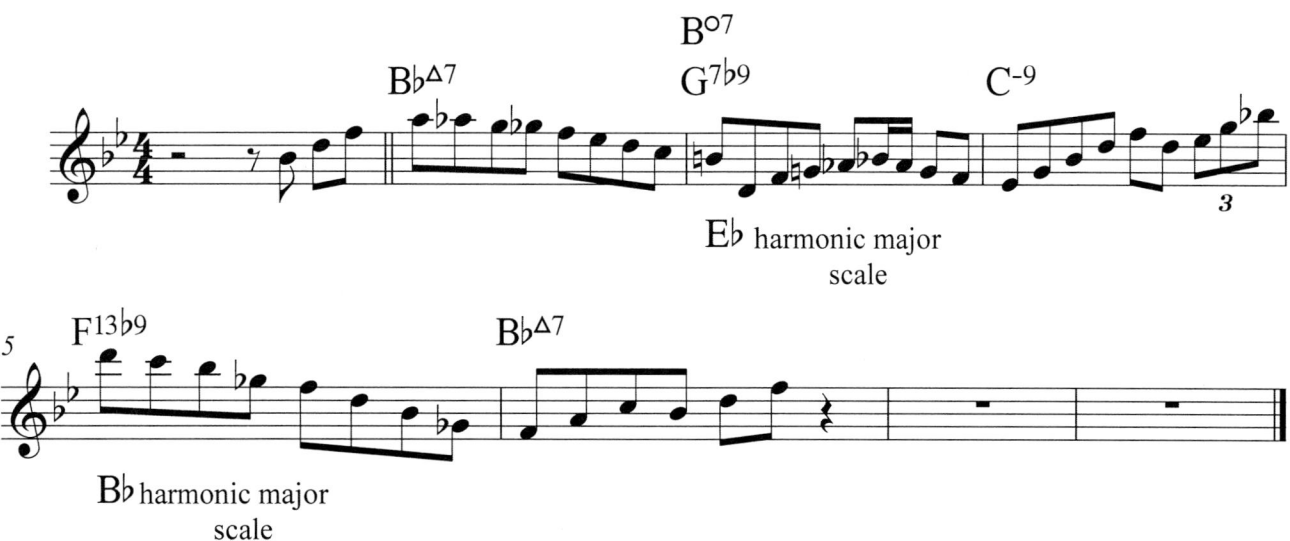

The last three examples showed how to deal with diminished chords on the flat 3 that descend by half-step to the ii chord. This example deals with a diminished chord on the ♯I ascending by half-step to the ii chord, in this case (in the key of B♭) a B°7 moving up to Cm7. This B diminished chord can be analyzed as a G7♭9, a secondary dominant (V of ii), and this G7 can be treated as a III chord from the E♭ harmonic major scale. The B♮ is the 3rd of G7 and the root of B°7 but it is actually the flat six of E♭ harmonic major and could have been written as a C♭ in this case. The B♭ in the line on the F13♭9 indicates that this is definitely a B♭ harmonic major scale and not a diminished scale.

Ex. 2.5 is another take on the same changes as in the last example and has the same analysis.

Ex. 2.5

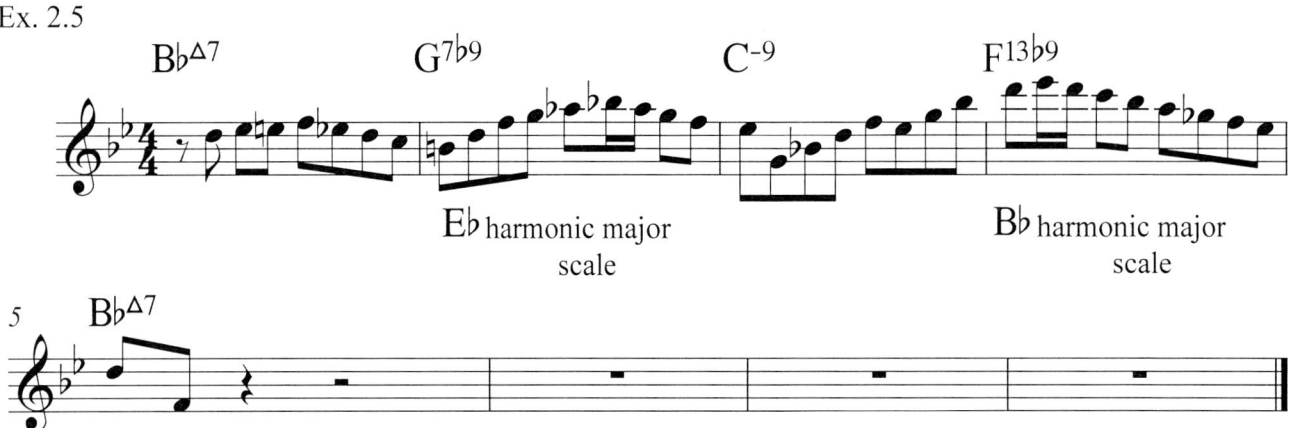

Ex. 2.6 shows a line based on the chord changes from the first five bars of the tune "I Remember Clifford."

Ex. 2.6

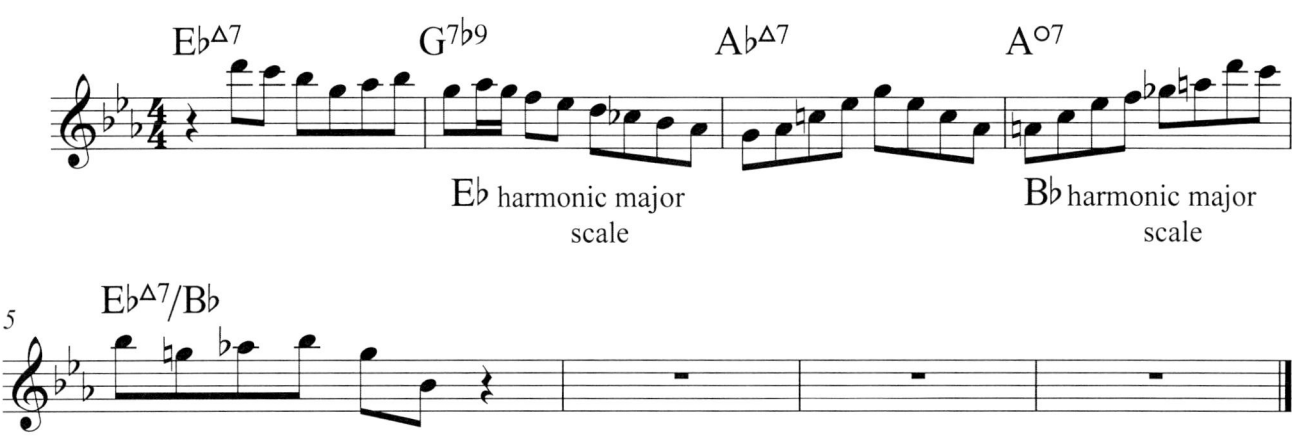

The G7♭9 is ordinarily the V of vi, a secondary dominant going to C minor, but here it progresses upward to A♭ major, the IV chord. Either way it can take the E♭ harmonic major scale. The A diminished chord, being symmetrical, can have any of its four notes act as the root, so it can be seen as being the same as the ♭3 diminished chord we analyzed earlier, and therefore the harmonic major scale on the 5th of the key (B♭) can be used.

Ex. 2.7 shows a line based on the chord changes from bars 9 through 13 from the tune "Alone Together."

CHAPTER 2 : SOME BASIC APPLICATIONS

Ex. 2.7

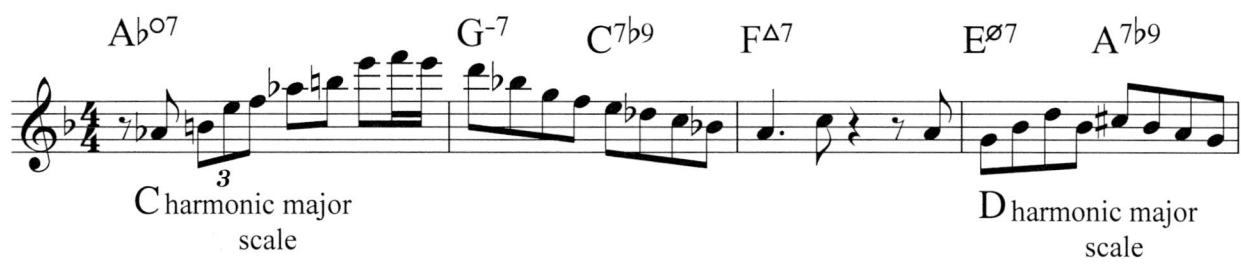

The A♭ diminished chord is from the original harmonization of the melody. The more usual contemporary fake book versions show this measure harmonized with B-7 to E7. This is actually a modern jazz re-harmonization reminiscent of the E-7 to A7 at the beginning of "Stella By Starlight" replacing the original B♭°7/D♭. So the scale is C harmonic major. Then the E⌀7 to A7♭9 going to D△7 implies the D harmonic major scale.

Harmonic major applied to some basic ii-V-I formulas
Ex. 2.8 shows the C harmonic major scale applied to some basic ii-V-I formulas demonstrating how lines connect chord changes.

Ex. 2.8

All of the notes in the example belong to the C harmonic major scale and all of the ii-V-Is shown use D⌀7 for the ii chord. To use the lines on ii-V-Is with D-7 as the ii chord simply replace any A♭ notes on the D⌀7 chords with A♮ notes. Each connection is shown in two versions, one "regular" and one with octave displacements, called "pivots" by Barry Harris. You should be able to work out dozens of variations by mixing and matching the two-beat four-note cells.

Using a harmonic major scale as a "skeleton" melody to add chromatics
Ex. 2.9 shows how the harmonic major scale can be used as a "skeleton" melody to which chromatics (such as approach notes and enclosures) can be added to create more interesting lines.

CHAPTER 2 : SOME BASIC APPLICATIONS

Ex. 2.9

The first four bars show a ii-V-I line that is the same as the first line from ex. 2.8, but written in quarter notes to form a longer "skeleton" phrase. All of the phrases that follow have those exact same notes on beats one, two, three, and four and with added chromatics on the "off" beats (the "ands"). Every four-note cell in the example can be swapped with any other four-note cell from the same part of the skeleton melody, so there are many variations waiting to be tried.

Using harmonic major scales to create chords and progressions in composition
The chords and chord movements found in the harmonic major scales can provide a great resource for harmonizing melodies and so can be very useful in composition. Ex. 2.10 shows an excerpt from a tune that uses harmonic major in places.

Ex. 2.10   R. Vincent

Bars four, five, and six use chords derived from the F harmonic major scale, namely C7♭9 (which in this tune can be voiced with a ♮11 along with the major 3rd), F△7, and B♭-△9. Bars seven and eight feature E♭△7♯5 (or E♭+△7) and B/A, both from the G harmonic major scale. The D♯ in the B/A is really E♭ from the G harmonic major scale. Bars nine, ten, eleven, and twelve are entirely from the D harmonic major scale. The D△7/B♭ could also be called B♭△7♯5♯9. The G-△9♯11 going to E⌀9 continues a cycle of descending thirds and, once again, the A7♭9 can be voiced with a ♮11 along with the major 3rd.

CHAPTER 3
"HIDDEN CHORDS" AND THE RELATIONSHIP TO "BEBOP" SCALES

The concept of "Hidden Chords"
The term "hidden chords" was used by Dan Greenblatt in *Minor is Major!*. It refers to diatonic harmonic structures present in a scale that are not the regular members of the tertian (derived from stacking thirds) triads or seventh chords, so therefore not obvious on first examination. We have already seen some above, such as the B major triad over A in ex. 2.10 and especially the almost completely altered dominant chord (7♭9♯9♭13 with a ♮5) built on the 3rd of the harmonic major scale. These hidden chords occur because in 21st century equal-tempered harmony enharmonic (means "sounds the same," such as A♭ sounds the same as G♯) notes can function in more than one way, so for example G♯ can be the major 3rd of E△7, the augmented 5th of C+7 "magically" changing into A♭ (the ♭13th) and then becomes the minor 3rd of F minor (see the last two bars of the bridge going to the first bar of the last A section in Kern's classic standard "All the Things You Are").

Using diatonic fourths to find "Hidden Chords"
Since hidden chords are not the usual expected tertian chords, one good way to start finding some would be to investigate diatonic harmonies derived from fourths (called "quartal harmony"). First let's check out the diatonic fourths that occur in the C harmonic major scale shown in ex. 3.1.

Ex. 3.1

Cmajor harmonic diatonic fourths

The fourths from C, D, G, and B are all perfect, while the fourths from F and A♭ are augmented. Finally, the fourth from E is diminished, which sounds like a major 3rd and can function as such.

Next check out Ex. 3.2, the diatonic quartal triads found in the C harmonic major scale.

Ex. 3.2

C harmonic major diatonic quartal triads

Some of these are difficult to give precise chord names to, starting with the C△7sus4 which has the 5th omitted. The Gsus4/D could also be called D7sus4 with the 5th omitted. The E7 looks mis-spelled, but remember that the A♭ can represent G♯. The Eomit3/F could also be called F△7♭5omit3. The Csus4/G could also be called G7sus4 with the 5th omitted. The Gomit3/A♭ could also be called A♭△7♭5omit3. Again the E/B uses A♭ to sound like G♯, the major 3rd of E.

Ex. 3.3 shows the C major harmonic diatonic quartal tetrads (four note chords).

Ex. 3.3

C harmonic major diatonic quartal tetrads

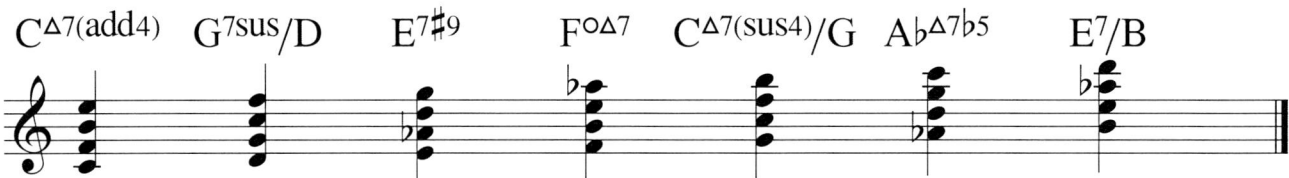

These names can be tricky too, but perhaps a little easier since they have four notes. The C△7add4 also has the 5th omitted. The G7sus4/D could also be called a D-7add4 with the 5th omitted. The E7♯9 again uses A♭ to sound like G♯. The F○△7 could also be called E/F. The C△7sus4/G could also be called G7add4omit5. The A♭△7♭5 actually has a ♯11 (the D♮), but this chord name is commonly used when the natural 5th is absent. By now I think you know the story for the E7/B.

As you can see, there are quite a few hidden chords in the harmonic major scale found just by using fourths instead of thirds. Many more are also possible and I'm not going to try to show them all here, so that can be a homework assignment. I do want to touch on a few more, however, that demonstrate an interesting phenomenon that I like to call "pseudo symmetries."

"Pseudo Symmetries"

This interesting phenomenon is probably more accurately called "pseudo parallels" but I liked the sound of pseudo symmetries better, so let's try to put up with it for a while. The way it works is that you take a chord voicing (could be regular or "hidden") and you move it up (or down) chromatically and at each half-step you check to see if it happens to contain all pitches present in the scale that generated the original voicing. In many cases this may result in actual parallels, such as D-7 and E-7 in a C major scale, or actual symmetries occurring in symmetrical scales, such as whole-tone and diminished scales. Pseudo symmetries happen when the structures are chromatically parallel but come from different diatonic configurations. Both the harmonic minor scale and the harmonic major scale have some good ones, but I'm going to stick to a few from harmonic major only. The rest are there waiting for you to discover.

CHAPTER 3 : "HIDDEN CHORDS" AND THE RELATIONSHIP TO "BEBOP" SCALES

Ex. 3.4 shows three examples of pseudo symmetries found in the C harmonic major scale.

Ex. 3.4

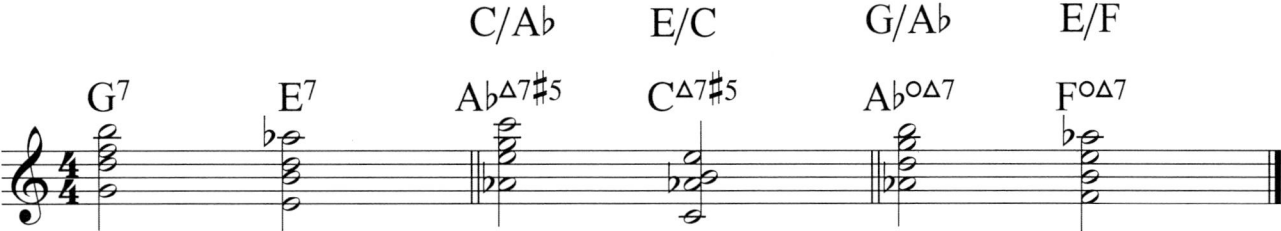

some "pseudo symmetries" found in C harmonic major

Although they are perfectly parallel in the chromatic scale, using the correct notation from the C harmonic major scale shows that they are not actually parallel structures diatonically speaking. Two of the examples show alternative chord names written as "slash" chords, or triads over bass notes. It should be noticed that both the G7 and the E7 could be expanded to G7b9 and E7b9, revealing some larger pseudo symmetries. Anyway this process of uncovering pseudo symmetries provides another way to reveal the presence of hidden chords. It also can be useful to see that when two parallel chords can be analyzed as a pseudo symmetry, the two chords can be seen as members of just one and the same scale, which you may find helpful as an aid in improvisation.

The "Bebop Scales" and the Barry Harris scales

In the early 1980s a student brought a book to the lesson that was written by David Baker. It introduced me to what Baker called "bebop scales." There were two that his method emphasized: the dominant bebop scale and the major bebop scale. Each was the standard scale with one added chromatic note, chosen so an improvisor could descend from any chord tone in eighth notes and keep the chord tones on the downbeats.

The dominant bebop scale (see Ex. 3.5) added a chromatic between the root and the ♭7th of the mixolydian scale, placing the tones of C7 on the beats.

Ex. 3.5

C dominant bebop scale

The major bebop scale (see Ex. 3.6) added a chromatic between the 6th and the 5th of the major scale, placing the tones of C6 on the beats.

Ex. 3.6

C major bebop scale

C7 has a whole-step between the root and the ♭7th, making it a good place for the added half-step, but C△7 only has a half-step between the root and △7th, so there's no room. Since C6 is compatible with C△7, the added half-step goes between the 6th and the 5th. This results in a "rule" suggested by Hal Galper and Jerry Bergonzi (among others) that any mode with a ♭7th can be made into a kind of bebop scale by adding the chromatic between the root and the ♭7th, and that any mode with a △7th can be made into a kind of bebop scale by adding the chromatic between the 6th and the 5th. This system works fine on the melodic minor scale, but both the harmonic minor and the harmonic major have △7ths and ♭6ths, so there's no room for chromatics at either location. Therefore the method doesn't produce the desired "bebop" result of chord tones on the beats for those scales. This is why I never thought of the bebop scale suggested by Dan Greenblatt on page 36 of *Minor is Major!* as a "bebop harmonic minor" scale (even though it contains all the notes of the harmonic minor scale). I had learned it as a natural minor bebop scale and knew that it has the same notes as its relative major bebop scale, so the A natural minor bebop scale has the same notes as the C major bebop scale. Matthieu's name of "utility minor" makes a lot of sense since it is so very useful (as we shall see).

Barry Harris dislikes the names "bebop scales," but teaches two of them using his own terminology. His view is that they are sources for harmony and chords rather than bebop line devices.

Ex. 3.7

"C major sixth-diminished seventh scale" or bebop major

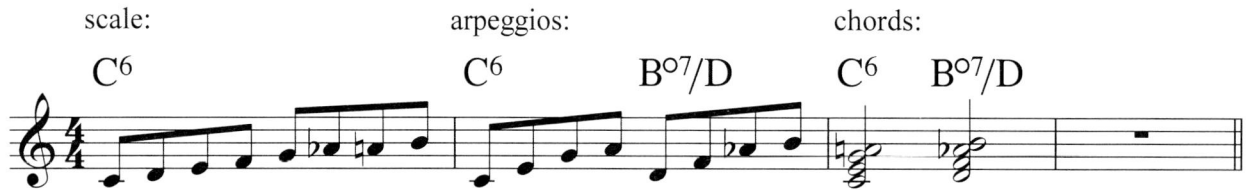

"A minor seventh-diminished seventh scale" or bebop natural minor

CHAPTER 3: "HIDDEN CHORDS" AND THE RELATIONSHIP TO "BEBOP" SCALES

Harris calls the major version the "major sixth-diminished seventh scale" and shows that it can be seen to be a major sixth chord with a passing diminished seventh chord sandwiched in between, shown in the top line of Ex. 3.7. Since C6 and A-7 have the same notes the relative minor version can be seen as a "minor seventh-diminished seventh scale," shown in the bottom line of Ex. 3.7.

In this case I have used G♯ rather than A♭ in order to comply with the chords and their functions, and you can see that it is the same as the A bebop natural minor scale, the A "Utility Minor" scale, and is the same as Dan Greenblatt's "bebop harmonic minor" scale. In the C major version the B diminished chord represents G7♭9, the dominant of C, while in the A minor version the G♯ diminished chord represents E7♭9, the dominant of A minor. All of the pitches sound the same.

Harris also teaches a minor version he calls the "minor sixth-diminished seventh scale," which is the same as what most jazz musicians now call the "melodic minor bebop scale." The chromatic is added between the 6th and 5th and it is a minor sixth chord with a passing diminished seventh chord sandwiched in between. One of the greatest contributions Harris has made is the realization that the sixth chords and the diminished chords can swap some notes, creating hybrids that vastly expand the palate of "hidden" chords that are available in our tonal system (more on this coming up soon).

The Relationship of Harmonic Major and the "Bebop" Scales

Let's take a look at the C major bebop scale, also called the A natural minor bebop scale and the C major sixth-diminished seventh scale. First of all, perhaps you have already noticed that the added note is A♭ or G♯, and therefore contains all of the notes found in the C harmonic major scale. This means that it contains not only all of the notes of C6 and B°7, but also all of the chords that are diatonic to the C major scale, and all of the chords that are diatonic to the C harmonic major scale, and yes, also all of the chords that are diatonic to the A harmonic minor scale since all the notes of that scale too are present. The major scale chords are C△7, D-7, E-7, F△7, G7, A-7, and B⌀7. The C harmonic major scale chords are C△7, D⌀7, E-7, F-△7, G7, A♭△7♯5, and B°7. The A harmonic minor scale chords are:
A-△7, B⌀7, C△7♯5, D-7, E7, F△7, and G♯°7. A couple of these are duplicates, but the majority offer a variety of harmonic choices. Also realize that all the "hidden" chords from these scales are also available.

Ex. 3.8 shows an application of Barry Harris' method of creating "hybrid" chords by swapping notes between the major sixth chord and the diminished seventh chord from the C major sixth-diminished seventh scale. I have chosen to spell all of the chromatic notes as A♭s for the sake of simplicity, even though in many cases using G♯ would be more compatible with the chord names. Many of the chord names are difficult to name precisely, and many have several alternate choices. I will try to mention some of them on the following page.

Ex. 3.8

C major sixth-diminished seventh scale:

$C^6 \quad B^{o7}/D \quad C^6/E \quad B^{o7}/F \quad C^6/G \quad B^{o7}/A\flat \quad C^6/A \quad B^{o7}$

one note swapped from each following chord:

$C^{\Delta 7} \quad D^{\varnothing 7} \quad A^{7sus}/E \quad F^{o\Delta 7} \quad F/G \quad A\flat^{o\Delta 7} \quad A^{-\Delta 7} \quad B^{\varnothing 7}$

two notes swapped from each following chord:

$C^{\Delta 7\sharp 5} \quad D^{-7} \quad E^{-7} \quad F^{-\Delta 7} \quad D^{-}/G \quad E^{-}/A\flat \quad F^{-}/A \quad G^{add9}/B$

three notes swapped from each following chord:

$C^{\Delta 7\sharp 5(sus4)} \quad D^{7sus} \quad E^7 \quad F^{\Delta 7} \quad G^7 \quad A\flat^{\Delta 7\sharp 5} \quad A^{\Delta 7\sharp 5(sus4)} \quad G^{6(add9)}/B$

Investigating this expanded collection of chords can help us to understand where so many of those puzzling "mystery" chords that sound so good come from.

CHAPTER 4
SOME PRACTICE SUGGESTIONS

Using "Minor is Major!" to create exercises for harmonic major scale practice

It is not my intention to re-write material that is already available, especially material that was so well written to begin with. I'm primarily referring to *Minor is Major!* by Dan Greenblatt again. If you don't already have a copy, then you should. I highly recommend it for his presentation of the importance of the harmonic minor scale in jazz and for his insightful commentaries on chord-scale theory and improvisation, and also especially for his Appendix: Getting Serious about Practicing Scales.

Also Appendix A in this book will present a series of practice patterns for the harmonic major scale that are mostly different from the ones in *Minor is Major!*, shown in one key only (C harmonic major) and in one octave only. Ex. 4.1 shows a sample for how using the Appendix from *Minor is Major!* to create exercises for harmonic major scale practice might be done.

Ex. 4.1

It is based on Exercise App.1 on page 127 of Greenblatt's book, which shows the E harmonic minor scale in thirds. Ex. 4.1 converts it into the C harmonic major scale in thirds. It's written in one octave only, but should be expanded to use the full range on your instrument. Of course it should also be learned and played in all keys. Again it's best if possible to work these out on your instrument without having to write them out. This same process can now be used for all of the scale studies in Greenblatt's Appendix. This may represent years of work, and you can't get it all done at once, so don't get discouraged. In fact you may never get it all mastered, but if you keep chipping away at it you will reap many positive results.

Using Barry Harris "pivots" to create exercises for harmonic major scale practice

Jazz great Barry Harris used the term "pivots" for seventh chord arpeggios that start on the root which has been raised by one octave, so they are really just 1-3-5-7 arpeggios that have been changed into 8-3-5-7 arpeggios.

Ex. 4.2 shows an old familiar melodic quote that has a pivot hidden inside, and also shows a literal example of a Barry Harris pivot.

Ex. 4.2

The quote is from the standard "Honeysuckle Rose" transposed into the key of C. It starts with an upper neighbor tone which displaces an F△7 pivot superimposed over a ii-V progression in C major. The literal Barry Harris pivot for F△7 is also shown. Both versions can be used to create exercises for harmonic major scale practice.

Ex. 4.3 shows the "Honeysuckle Rose" quote adjusted to fit each step of the C harmonic major scale.

Ex. 4.3

Ex. 4.4 shows the Barry Harris pivots applied to the C harmonic major scale. The outlined chords naturally descend in thirds, so the second four bars show the outlined chords that were skipped in the first four bars.

Ex. 4.4

Using quartal triads and tetrads to create "hidden" arpeggios
Just as we used quartal harmony to discover hidden chords in Chapter 3, we can now use those same chords to demonstrate the creation of hidden arpeggios that can be useful for single-note improvisation.

Ex. 4.5 shows the diatonic quartal triad arpeggios that are derived directly from the chords shown in Ex. 3.2.

Ex. 4.5

quartal triad arpeggios found in
the C harmonic major scale:

You can use the names from 3.2 to analyze the arpeggios, but I didn't repeat them here because these arpeggios may be used in many ways over any chords that can be analyzed as subsets of the C harmonic major scale. Try them out, and any you don't like, don't use, but you may find many unexpected applications that are surprisingly good.

Ex. 4.6 shows a practice routine that should be applied to each arpeggio shown in 4.5. It uses the first arpeggio to demonstrate and you can repeat each section as many times as needed.

Ex. 4.6

practice routine to be applied to
each quartal triad found in the
Charmonic major scale:

CHAPTER 4 : SOME PRACTICE SUGGESTIONS

Ex. 4.7 shows the diatonic quartal tetrad arpeggios that are derived directly from the chords shown in Ex. 3.3. Again I am skipping the names and leaving the applications wide open.

Ex. 4.7

quartal tetrad arpeggios found in
the C harmonic major scale:

Ex. 4.8 shows a practice routine that should be applied to each arpeggio shown in 4.7. Again it uses the first arpeggio to demonstrate and you can repeat each section as many times as needed.

Ex. 4.8

practice routine to be applied to
each quartal tetrad found in the
C harmonic major scale:

Some pentatonic scales that are subsets of the harmonic major scale
Ex. 4.9 shows seven possible pentatonic scales that are subsets of the C harmonic major scale. Some possible names are shown. Some of them are also subsets of other more familiar scales and so you may already be familiar with those. I'll mention a few. The Dø7add11 is also F-6add9. The E7#9 uses A♭ for G♯ and has a ♭5. The G7add4 is what I sometimes referred to as "the Beatles scale" because it reminded me of the tuning of a sitar that I heard on a Beatles recording from the 1960s. The A♭+∆7#11 is the same as a C major pentatonic scale with a ♭6. B°7add11 has the exact same notes as E7♭9 with a ♮5.

CHAPTER 4 : SOME PRACTICE SUGGESTIONS

Ex. 4.9

some pentatonic scales that are subsets of
the C harmonic major scale:

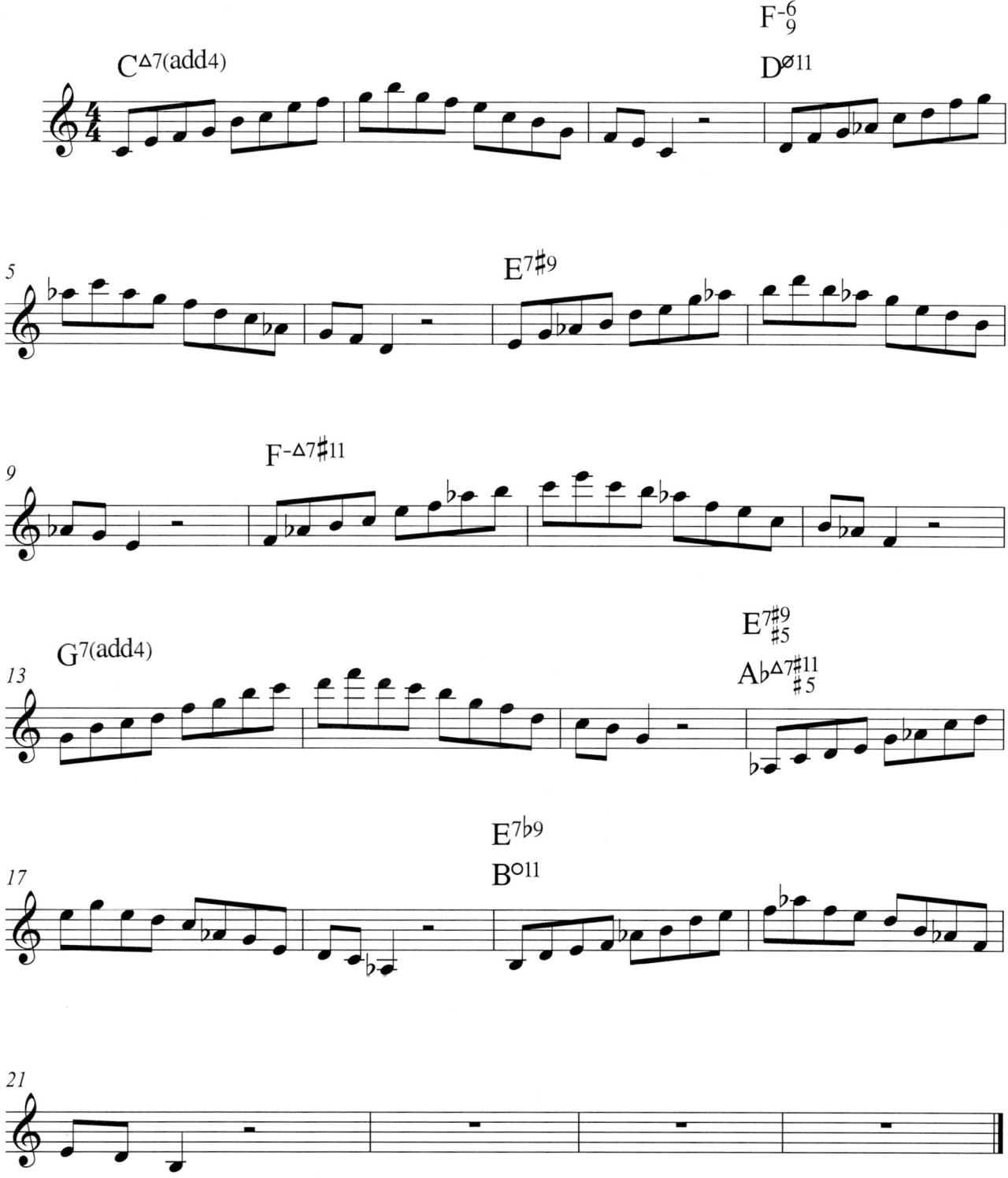

Deriving arpeggios from Barry Harris hybrid chords

Useful arpeggios can also be derived from those hybrid chords with swapped notes from the Barry Harris major sixth-diminished seventh scale. The harmonic major scale is a subset, but the full Barry Harris scale in C major also has the note A♮, so some of the chords and arpeggios (namely all those that contain the A♮ note) are not diatonic to C harmonic major, while all of those that do not have the A♮ note are. I'm including them all for the sake of completeness.

Ex. 4.10 shows the hybrid arpeggios for the chords shown in the second line of ex. 3.8, the chords with one swapped note.

Ex. 4.10

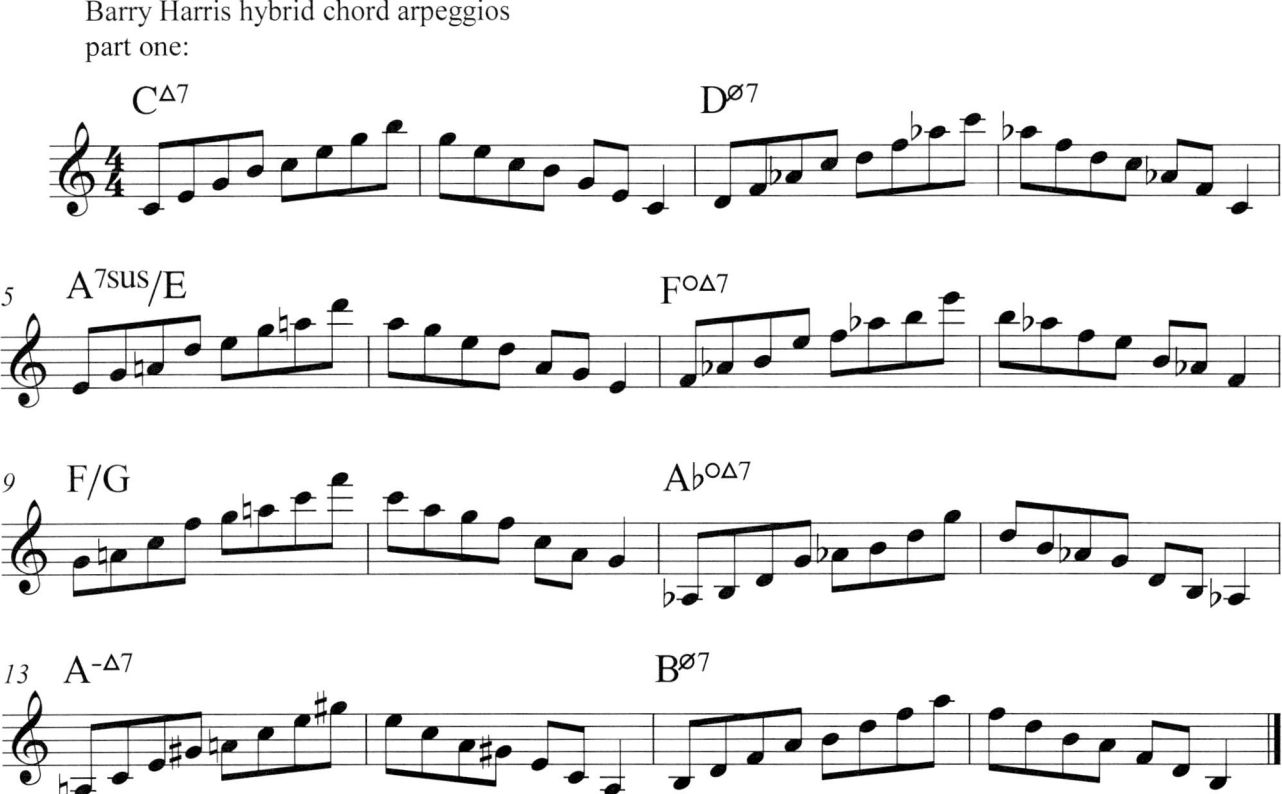

Ex. 4.11 shows the hybrid arpeggios for the chords shown in the third line of ex. 3.8, the chords with two swapped notes.

Ex. 4.11

Barry Harris hybrid chord arpeggios
part two:

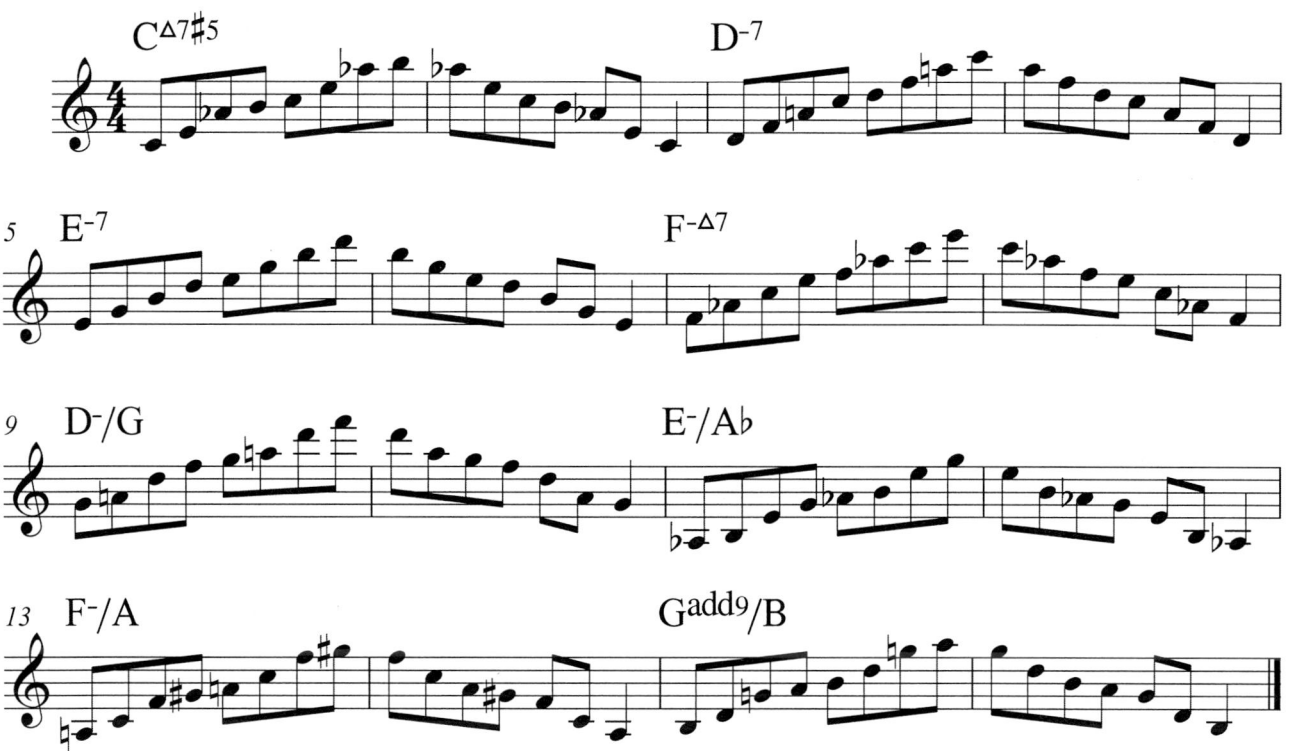

Ex. 4.12 shows the hybrid arpeggios for the chords shown in the bottom line of ex. 3.8, the chords with three swapped notes.

Ex. 4.12

Next I would like to share a few more thoughts about these so-called "bebop scales."

CHAPTER 5
SOME THOUGHTS ABOUT BEBOP SCALES

A Charlie Parker melodic minor bebop line
Ex. 5.1 shows a line from a Charlie Parker solo that fits nicely over a common sub-dominant minor to tonic major progression in the key of F. It happens over a B♭-6 to E♭7 to F△7.

Ex. 5.1

Charlie Parker

The basic parent scale for the B♭-6 to E♭7 is B♭ melodic minor, so the B♭-6 can have a △7th and a ♮9th and the E♭7 has a ♮9th, a ♯11th, and a ♮13th (E♭ lydian dominant). This example was chosen because it shows Parker playing an entire descending B♭ bebop melodic minor scale in the 2nd measure. Like the major bebop scale it has an added chromatic note between the 6th and 5th steps of the parent scale, the note G♭ in this case. It is the same as the Barry Harris "minor sixth-diminished seventh" scale.

This scale conforms to the "rule" suggested by Hal Galper and Jerry Bergonzi that any mode with a ♭7th can be made into a kind of bebop scale by adding the chromatic between the root and the ♭7th, and that any mode with a △7th can be made into a kind of bebop scale by adding the chromatic between the 6th and the 5th. Since the melodic minor scale has a △7th the chromatic note is added between the 6th and the 5th.

Bebop scales derived from modes of the major scale
Now let's check out the bebop scales that result from applying the "rule" to the seven modes of the major scale. Ex. 5.2 shows the modes and corresponding bebop scales derived from the C major scale.

Ex. 5.2

modes and bebop scales derived from the C major scale:

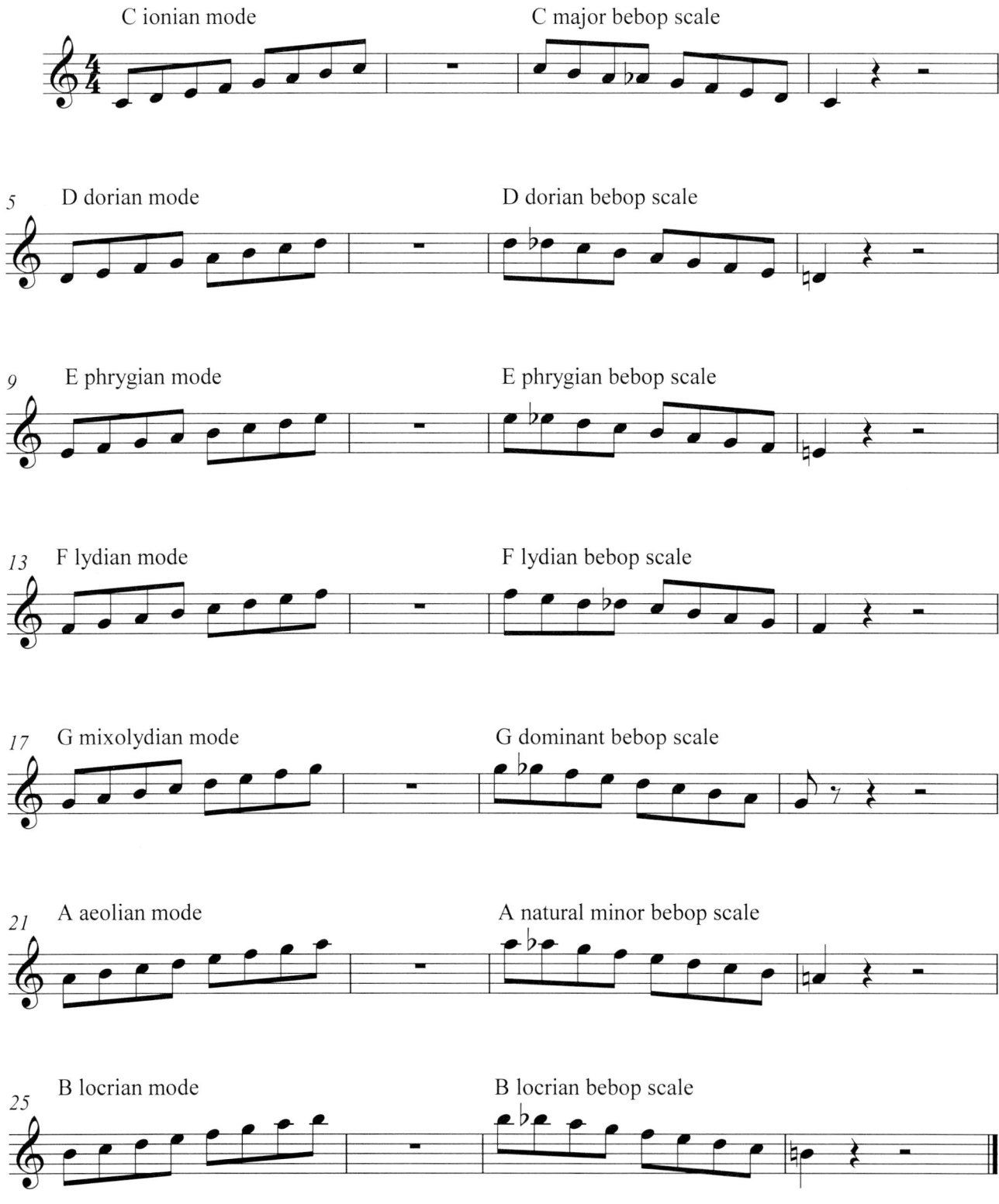

CHAPTER 5 : SOME THOUGHTS ABOUT BEBOP SCALES

The left side shows one ascending octave of each diatonic mode. The right side shows how each mode can be converted into a descending bebop scale by adding one chromatic note to each mode according to the "rule." For convenience I've used the commonly used Greek names for the modes and also for the bebop variations. In order to understand their application let's check out a broad overview of the diatonic seventh chords in C major and their functionality.

A simplified overview of tonality
Ex. 5.3 shows the diatonic seventh chords in the key of C major, but divided into two groups labeled as "resolving chords" and "tension chords."

Ex. 5.3

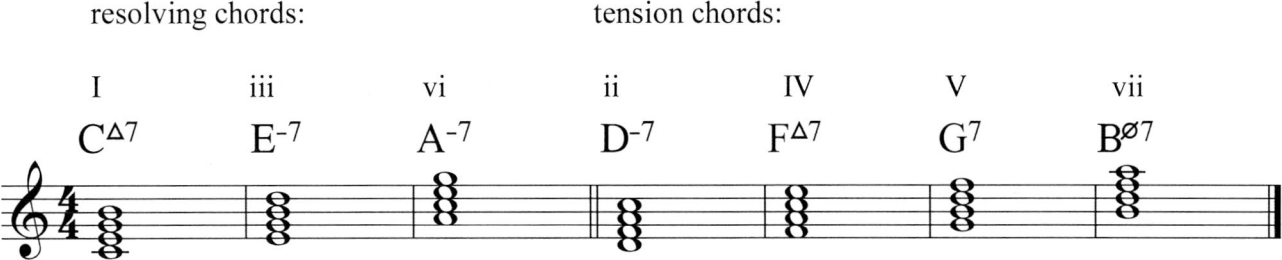

In the resolving group are the I7 (C△7), the iii7 (E-7), and the vi7 (A-7), which contain only notes that are compatible with the Tonic function. In the tension group are the ii7 D-7), the IV7 (F△7), the V7 (G7), and the vii7 (Bø7), all of which contain the note F, which is the only diatonic note in C major that is absolutely not compatible with the Tonic function.

Referring back to ex. 5.2 we notice that the F notes in the major bebop scale, the phrygian bebop scale, and in the natural minor bebop scale are merely passing tones that are "off" the beat, while the F notes that are in the dorian bebop scale, the lydian bebop scale, the dominant bebop scale, and the locrian bebop scale are all "on" the beat, making the F notes sound like harmonic target notes. Notice that the notes in the C major bebop scale are the same as the notes in the A natural minor bebop scale. This is also true for the D dorian bebop scale and the the F lydian bebop scale. All of the bebop scales related to the resolving chords are interchangeable over any of those resolving chords, and, yes, all of the bebop scales related to the tension chords are interchangeable over any of those tension chords. To demonstrate this concept let's look at a couple of examples.

Ex. 5.4 shows a D "dorian" bebop scale as taught in most contemporary jazz improvisation methods.

Ex. 5.4

D "dorian" bebop scale:

G dominant bebop scale:

Notice it doesn't follow the "rule." Instead of adding a chromatic note between the the root and the "7th the added chromatic passing tone is a major 3rd between the minor 3rd and the 4th. Notice that the notes are the same as the notes from the G dominant bebop scale shown just below. Many of the bebop era jazz musicians did actually view the ii-V chord progression as one unified sound unless they wanted to use altered sounds on the dominant chord.

Ex. 5.5 shows a minor tonality ii-V-i in A minor, the relative minor of C major.

Ex. 5.5

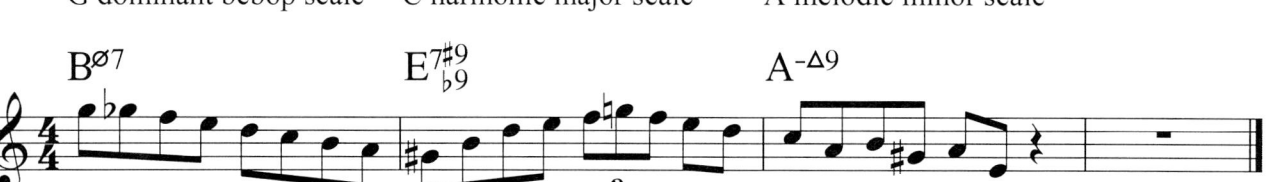

So now the B⌀7 is a ii rather than a vii, followed by E7 as the V and A-∆9 as the I. This is a line similar to ones taught by Barry Harris as Charlie Parker inspired lines for minor tonality cadences. Harris, who disliked the term "bebop scale," called the G dominant bebop scale a G dominant 7th scale with an added chromatic passing tone. Once again the idea of using the G dominant bebop scale for the B⌀7, another one of the "tension" chords, is demonstrated.

CHAPTER 5 : SOME THOUGHTS ABOUT BEBOP SCALES

Introducing ninth chord bebop scales
It follows that some of these bebop "modes" can be thought of and used as ninth chord bebop scales. Ex. 5.6 shows how this works with C△9.

Ex. 5.6

E phrygian bebop scale or Cmaj9 bebop scale:

First it shows a C△9 chord, then an E-7 chord. It's easy to see that the E-7 chord is the 3rd, 5th, 7th, and 9th of the C△9 chord. Since the E phrygian bebop scale outlines the notes of an E-7 chord in the key of C major, it seems that the scale can be used over the C△9 chord. To my ear a phrygian mode implies a sus♭9 sound rather than a -7 sound, so I prefer to think of the bebop scale shown in 5.6 as a C△9 bebop scale.

Let's see if the same concept will work for G9. Ex. 5.7 first shows a G9 chord, then a Bø7 chord.

Ex. 5.7

B locrian bebop scale or G9 bebop scale:

Once again it's easy to see that the Bø7 chord is the 3rd, 5th, ♭7th, and 9th of the G9 chord. The B locrian bebop scale shown in 5.7 outlines the notes of a Bø7 chord in the key of C major, so while it is fine for the Bø7 chord, it is also a great G9 bebop scale.

Ten-note bebop scales
Another thing to try is adding more chromatics by following this "rule": where there is a diatonic major 3rd divided into two whole-steps you can fill it in with the extra chromatics, resulting in what we might think of as ten-note bebop scales. It works especially well when descending, so our examples will do just that. Ex. 5.8 demonstrates.

Ex. 5.8

ten-note bebop scales

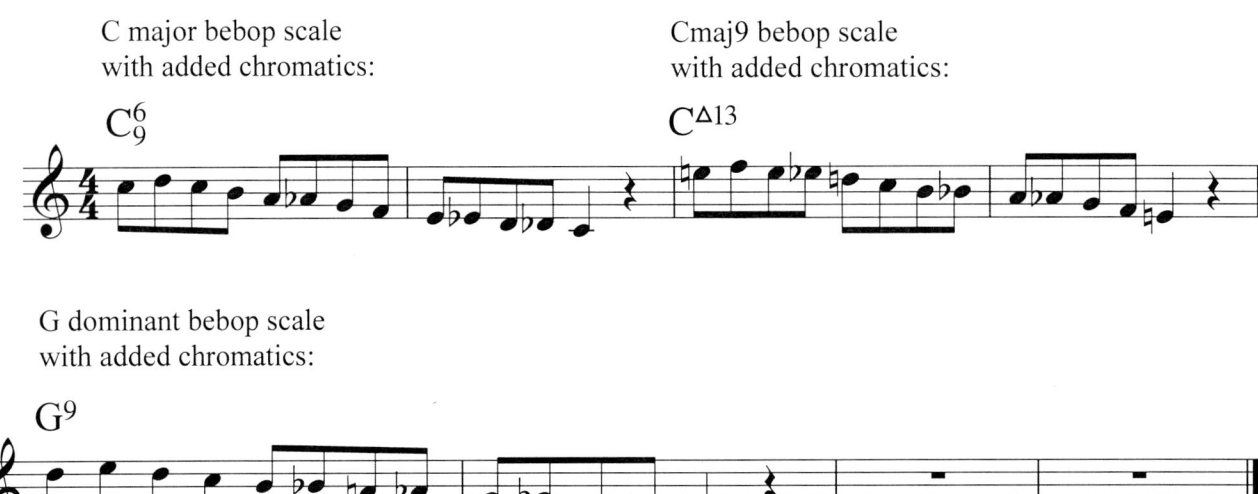

The C major bebop scale has a major 3rd divided into two whole-steps, the E down to C with the D in between, so that is where the extra chromatics are added. The C△9 bebop scale has a major 3rd from B down to G with the A in between, so there we've added the extra chromatics. The G dominant bebop scale also has the major 3rd from B down to G with the A in between, so again that is where we find the added chromatics. The G9 bebop scale has the major 3rd from A down to F with the G in between, so when we add the chromatics it is the same as the the G dominant bebop scale with added chromatics, so there is only one ten-note dominant bebop scale derived from the major scale modes.

Bebop scales derived from the modes of the melodic minor scale
Now let's try what we did with the major scale modes, but this time applied to the modes of the melodic minor scale. Ex. 5.9 shows the modes and corresponding bebop scales derived from the C melodic minor scale.

CHAPTER 5 : SOME THOUGHTS ABOUT BEBOP SCALES

Ex. 5.9

modes and bebop scales derived from the C melodic minor scale:

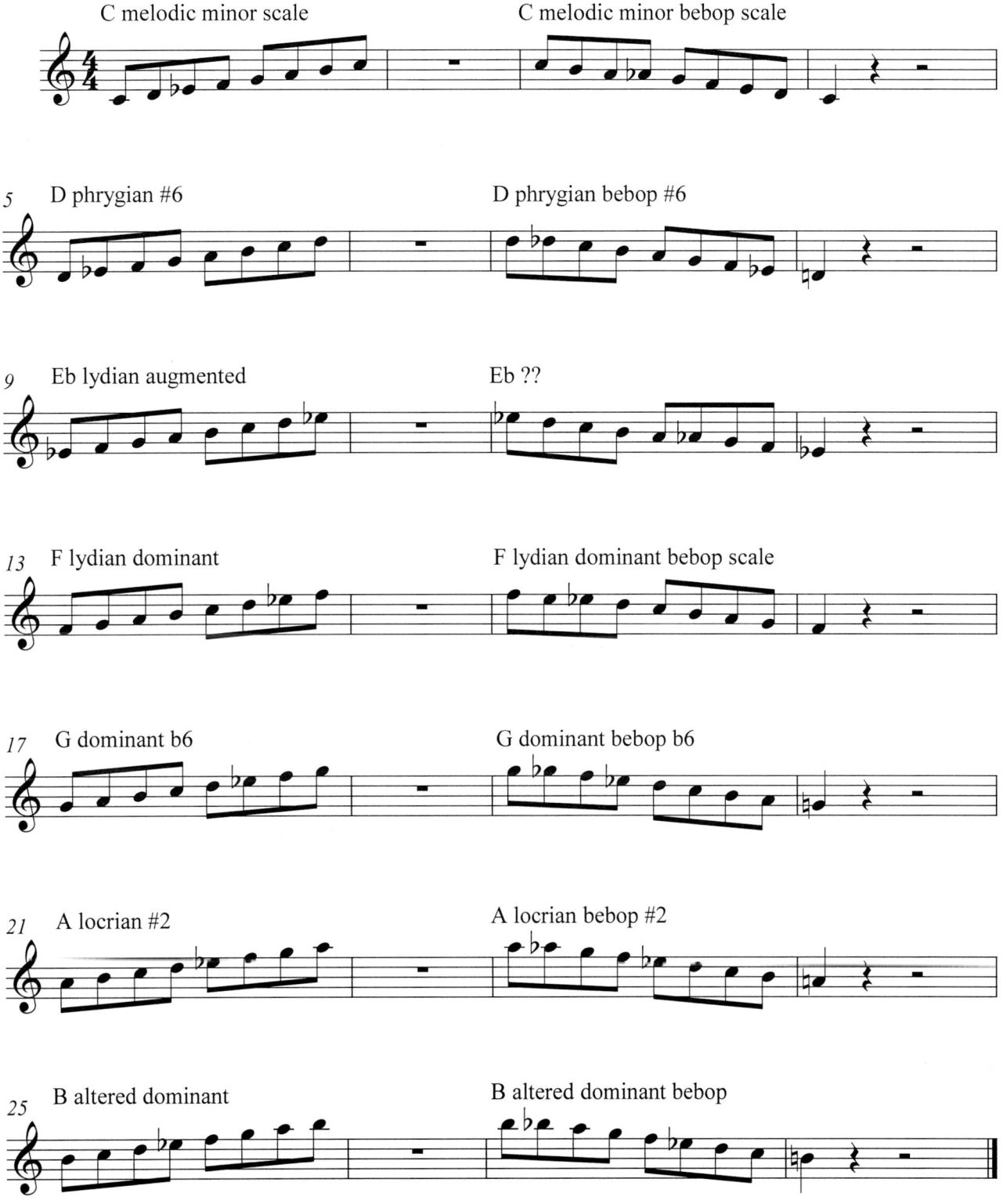

The left side shows one ascending octave of each diatonic mode. The right side shows how each mode can be converted into a descending bebop scale by adding one chromatic note to each mode according to the "rule." Let's check them out in order.

The melodic minor bebop scale shown is the same as the one played by Charlie Parker in ex. 5.1, only in C minor rather than B♭ minor. The D phrygian ♯6 is usually called dorian ♭2 in most jazz methods since it is the second mode of the parent scale. I prefer phrygian ♯6 because it generates a D13sus♭9 chord, which sounds much more phrygian than dorian. I know that the ♯6 is really a ♮6 (B♮ in this case), but the sharp is just relative to the usual note at that spot in the mode. The E♭ lydian augmented presents a problem: since it has both a △7th and a ♯5th the "rule" cannot be applied. The best solution I have found is to treat it as an inversion of the first mode, so the notes are the same as in the C melodic minor bebop scale. This outlines an E♭6♭5, which is compatible with E♭△7♯5. The passing notes in the G dominant bebop ♭6 outline a diminished 7th chord and makes it the same scale that Barry Harris calls the "dominant seventh-diminished seventh" scale. The A locrian ♮2 (could also be called A aeolian ♭5) is a popular contemporary mode for use on a A⌀7 chord. Since A⌀7 has exactly the same notes as C-6, the A locrian bebop ♮2 scale has exactly the same notes as the C melodic minor bebop scale. The altered dominant bebop scale isn't as commonly used because it outlines a B°7 chord, which is compatible with a B altered dominant chord, but not as good (in my opinion) as outlining C-6 again, which has the 3rd, the ♭7th, the ♭9th, and the ♭13th of the B altered dominant chord. Feel free to experiment with any or all of these, but for me the fact that all the chords and modes of the melodic minor scale are compatible (and therefore somewhat interchangeable) my go-to choice is the melodic minor bebop scale.

The ten-note melodic minor bebop scale

Now let's try adding more chromatics to the melodic minor bebop scale following the "rule" where there is a diatonic major 3rd divided into two whole-steps you can fill it in with the extra chromatics, resulting in what we have been calling a ten-note bebop scale. It works especially well when descending, so our example will do just that. Ex. 5.10 demonstrates.

Ex. 5.10

ten-note melodic minor bebop scale

C melodic minor bebop scale
with added chromatics:

Bebop scales and lines related to the harmonic major scale

When looking to apply the "rule" creating bebop scales to the harmonic major scale we instantly encounter a great difficulty because, having a △7th and a ♭6th the "rule" cannot be applied. The augmented 2nd and the three minor 2nds make most of the hoped for bebop scales impractical. The dominant 7th chord in any scale will always yield a potentially useful bebop scale.

CHAPTER 5 : SOME THOUGHTS ABOUT BEBOP SCALES

I will also show one built from the third mode that to my ear seems to have some potential. Ex. 5.11 shows them both.

Ex. 5.11

Ex. 5.12 shows a line the has a bebop scale-like quality and is a subset of the C harmonic major scale with added chromatics filling the major 3rd between the E and the C (divided into two whole-tones by the D).

Ex. 5.12

bebop style line that is a subset of
the C harmonic major scale:

It outlines a Cadd9 chord in the context of C harmonic major. It forms an eight note bebop-like scale because the B is omitted. This is just one example of the type of thing you can experiment with.

Bebop scales and lines related to the harmonic minor scale

The harmonic minor scale is perhaps even more difficult than the harmonic major for deriving useful bebop scales, and for basically the same reasons. As mentioned previously, the dominant 7th chord in any scale will always yield a potentially useful bebop scale, so that's what we'll look at here. Ex. 5.13 shows the fifth mode of the C harmonic minor scale, usually called G mixolydian ♭2 ♭6.

Ex. 5.13

It's a match for G7♭9♭13, also sometimes called G7♯5♭9. The G dominant bebop ♭2 ♭6 scale is formed by adding the usual chromatic note between the root and the ♭7th. Jerry Bergonzi recommends this scale for both the ii chord (D⌀7 in this key) and the V chord (G7 in this key), covering the ii-V progression before changing to the melodic minor bebop scale for the I chord (C-6 in this key).

Ex. 5.14 shows a line that has a bebop scale-like quality and is a subset of the C harmonic minor scale with added chromatics filling the major 3rd between the G and the E♭ (divided into two whole-tones by the F).

Ex. 5.14

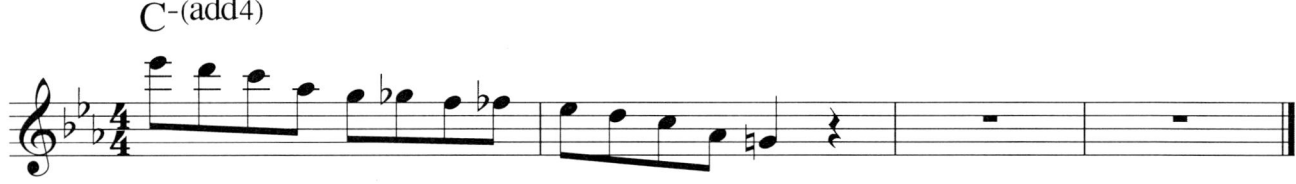

It outlines a C-add4 chord in the context of C harmonic minor. It forms an eight note bebop-like scale because the B is omitted. Again this is just one example of the type of thing you can experiment with.

Another thing I would like to explore is a different way to think about how to use so-called "cells" in jazz improvisation.

CHAPTER 6:
A DIFFERENT APPROACH TO IMPROVISING USING CELLS

The basic concept

The usual approach to cellular improvisation as taught by Jerry Bergonzi, Hal Galper, and as I presented in my own books on the topic, is to use small (usually two beats long) melodic fragments that are strung together into longer flowing lines. This is often to accommodate fast moving (usually two beats each) chord changes, where it makes a whole lot of sense. They can also be strung together over longer slower moving changes, and also over static harmonies as in modal situations, or even for "free" improvisations. The new approach that I am now suggesting is to take existing longer lines from bebop melodies and from recorded solos and breaking them apart into smaller cellular fragments that can then be re-assembled into a variety of longer lines that are not just verbatim quotes but that share the same vocabulary as the great jazz masters.

One important concept to grasp is the idea that each two-beat cell has a specific target note that completes the function of that cell. Occasionally there may be two or even three different possible targets, but the cells have a strong tendency to only sound correct when followed by an appropriate target tone. Ex. 6.1 illustrates.

Ex. 6.1

These are two cells shown with their target notes. The cell for A7b9 is also good for C#°7 going to D minor. Both of these cells were derived from longer lines which will be shown, although they may be in different keys. This brings up another important point; the cells, once extracted from the original source, should be practiced in all keys in addition to being joined together with other appropriate cells.

Deriving some cells from a famous bebop tune

Ex. 6.2 shows a brief passage from the well-known bebop tune "Donna Lee," along with two cells extracted and shown with their target notes.

Ex. 6.2

The cell shown in measure three has a chromatic enclosure of the target tone B♭, the chord root in this case. It does not imply either a ᴬ7 or a ♭7, so it can be applied to either B♭ᴬ7 or to B♭7.

The cell shown in measure four is the famous "Honeysuckle Rose" quote. It can imply F-7 with an 11th and a 9th, or it can imply A♭ᴬ7, a common superimposition for B♭7 which suggests B♭13sus4.

Ex. 6.3 shows another short fragment from "Donna Lee" that shows the Dø7 arpeggio used to outline 3, 5, ♭7, and 9 of a B♭9 chord.

Ex. 6.3

This cell can target the 13th as in the original version. Measures three and four show the same cell with an alternate target as played in a solo by saxophone great George Coleman. Coleman did it in a different key but I transposed it to demonstrate the similarities and differences. Beats three and four of bar three is another highly useful cell with its only target note on beat one of bar four.

Deriving some more cells from some recorded jazz solos
Ex. 6.4 shows the opening two bars of a brilliant solo recorded by guitarist Hank Garland on a slow ballad (hence the sixteenth notes).

Ex. 6.4

Notice that the first four notes are the same 3-5-♭7-9 arpeggio shown in ex. 6.3, but in a new key. Also notice the new target note. This cell seems to have several good targets. Next I've derived cells from the example, but changed into eighth notes for more general use.

CHAPTER 6: A DIFFERENT APPROACH TO IMPROVISING USING CELLS

The cell in bar four is a bebop scale fragment and has only one likely target note.

The cell in bar five can work for C-7 or Eb△7 as well as for F7.

The cell shown in bar six on the E7 is a very common bit of jazz vocabulary, as we will see. The target note is the 3rd of the chord. The cell, however, has no 7th and again can imply either a △7 chord or a dominant 7 chord.

Ex. 6.5 shows a two cell fragment and its target note. It was extracted from a trumpet solo by Clifford Brown.

Ex. 6.5

from a Clifford Brown solo:

Perhaps you may have noticed that this is actually a re-combination of two cells we've already looked at (although in a different key), so it's a perfect example of the cellular re-combination process that I've been talking about. The first cell (shown in bar three) is exactly the same as the last cell from 6.4, but transposed. The second cell (shown in bar four) is exactly the same as the first cell from 6.2 and again, transposed. The F♯ note is part of a chromatic enclosure of the root G, so even though the chord is G△7 the cell can also be used effectively on a G7 chord.

Ex. 6.6 shows another two cell fragment with target note. It was extracted from a guitar solo by Wes Montgomery.

Ex. 6.6

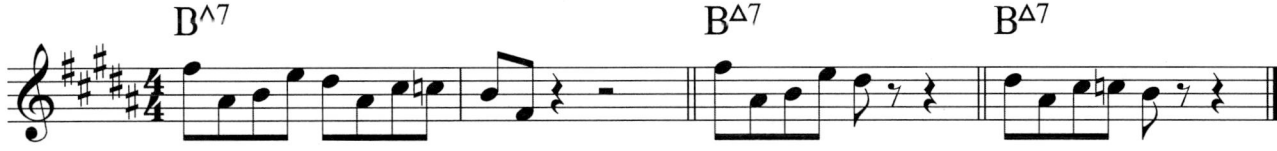

from a Wes Montgomery solo:

The key of B major is very unusual in jazz, but Wes was not only a genius, but also a guitarist, so keys didn't really matter to him. I suggest learning it in a more familiar key first, then of course transpose into all keys. These cells are completely interchangeable with the cells from 6.5 since they start on and target the same relative notes, emphasizing the 5th, the 3rd, and the root of the chord.

Okay, I think I will show the rest of the examples written in the key of B♭. It should be easier for most and using the same key will make many of the re-combinations easier when we get to them.

Ex.6.7 shows a line from a Joe Pass guitar solo that he played over a △7 chord. I'm showing it in the key of B♭ major. It sounds to me like it would be just as good in G minor over a G-9 chord.

Ex. 6.7
from a Joe Pass solo:

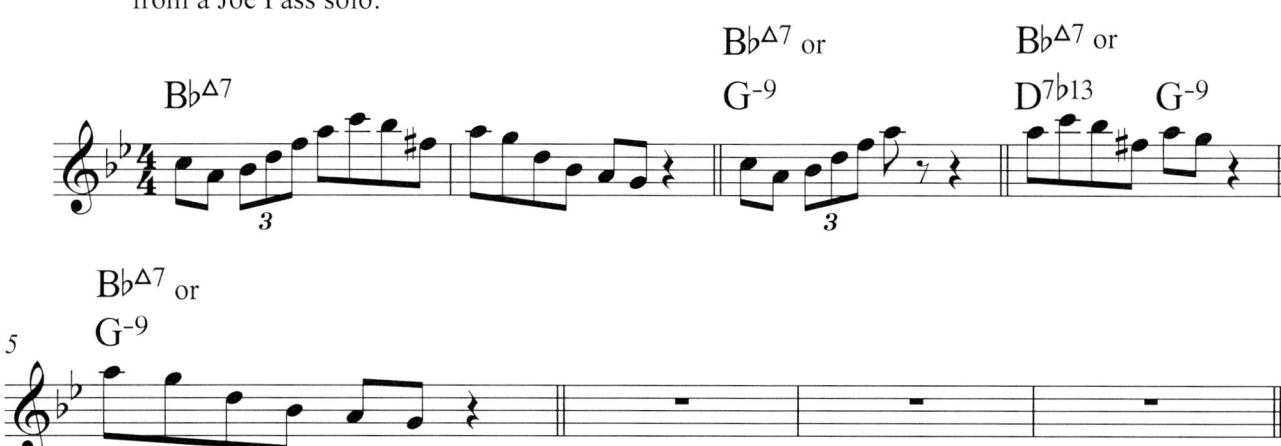

The first cell has five notes in two beats and uses a triplet.

The second cell, isolated in bar four, shows the harmonic implication of a V-i progression in G minor, even though Pass played it over a simple B♭△7 chord. To my ear this cell needs two eighth notes to create a satisfactory target, so they are shown.

The last cell, isolated in bar five, is the famous "Cry Me A River" quote (so famous, in fact, that many jazz educators call it "CMAR" for short), outlining a G minor triad with an added 9th. To my ear this cell also needs two eighth notes to create a satisfactory target, so both are shown here.

Ex. 6.8 shows another line from Joe Pass.

Ex. 6.8
from a Joe Pass solo:

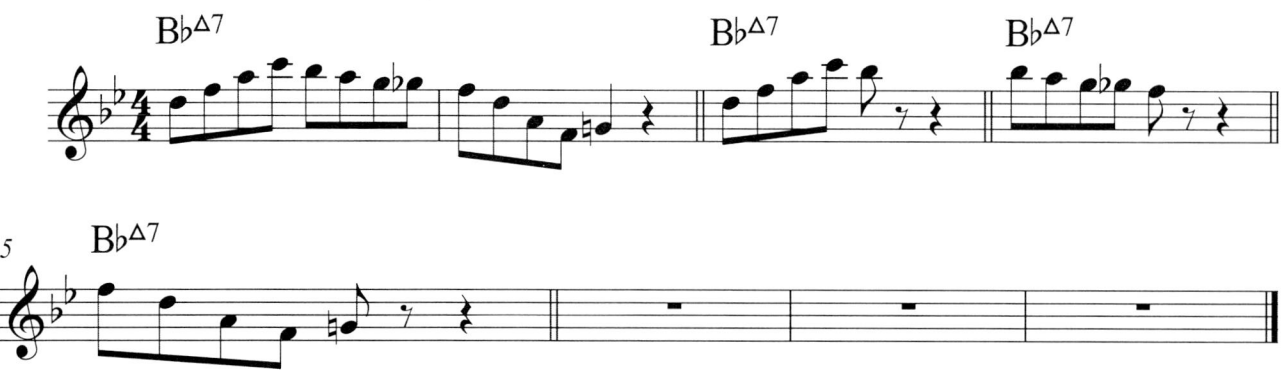

CHAPTER 6 : A DIFFERENT APPROACH TO IMPROVISING USING CELLS

The first cell, isolated in bar three, is a D-7 arpeggio outlining 3-5-7-9 of Bb△7.

The second cell, isolated in bar four, descends a portion of the Bb major bebop scale.

The third cell, isolated in bar five, descends the D minor triad portion of Bb△7, and nicely targets the 6th.

Ex. 6.9 shows a line from Charlie Parker.

Ex. 6.9

from a Charlie Parker solo:

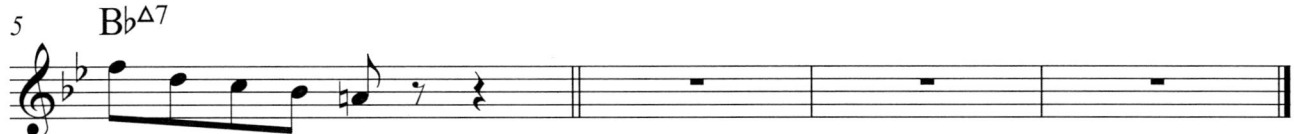

The first cell starts off the beat on the "and" of one and proceeds with a triplet, so it's still four notes. It could have been played in all eighth notes starting on beat one, but Parker gives it an extra "kick" with this syncopation.

The next cell descends chromatically from the 7th down to the 5th.

The last cell is a reversed 1-2-3-5 cell, so it's 5-3-2-1 followed by a melody reminiscent of the end of 6.8.

Ex. 6.10 is another passage from a Charlie Parker solo.

Ex. 6.10

from a Charlie Parker solo:

It starts with the first measure being identical to the first bar of 6.9, so we won't rehash those cells. The first new cell is isolated in bar five, a descending line connecting the 3rd of D⌀7 to the 3rd of G7b9.

The next new cell is identical (but transposed) to the second cell shown in 6.1 at the beginning of this chapter.

The last two cells are all notes from an Eb∆7 arpeggio, which spells out b3-5-b7-9 of a C-9 chord. The C target note at the end is only one good choice among several possibilities, so please experiment.

Ex. 6.11 shows a long flowing ii-V-I line from a Joe Pass guitar solo.

Ex. 6.11

from a Joe Pass solo:

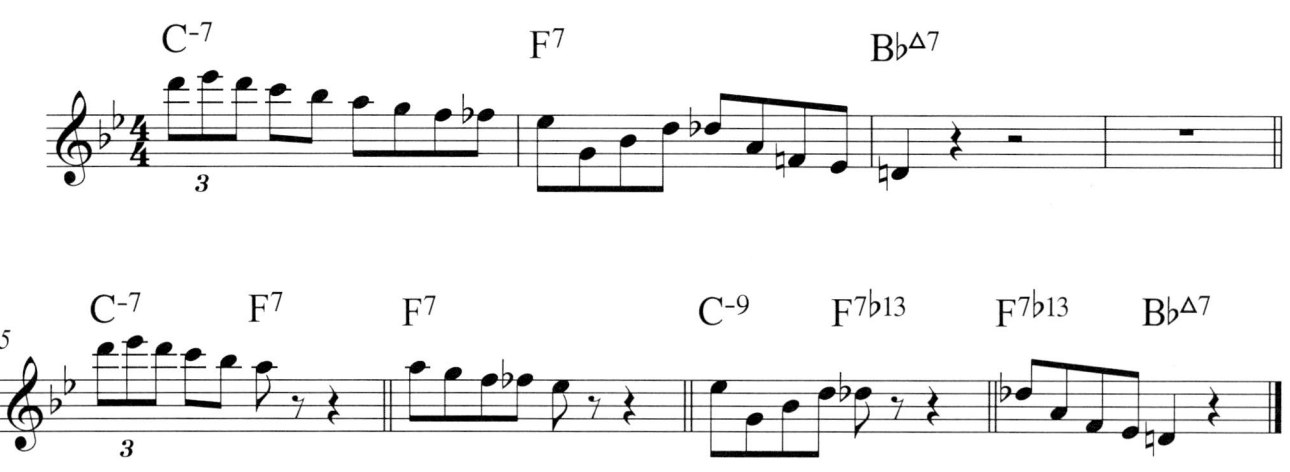

Even though the line was played over a straight ii-V-I, isolating the cells shows the detailed harmonic implications that can take place inside such a passage.

CHAPTER 6 : A DIFFERENT APPROACH TO IMPROVISING USING CELLS

The first cell is isolated in bar five and implies C-7 going to F7.

The second cell, isolated in bar six, is a descending F dominant bebop scale fragment that we already saw in 6.4 from Hank Garland.

The third cell, isolated in bar seven, implies C-9 going to F7b13, with the classic 9 to b13 voice leading.

The last cell, isolated in bar eight, has the expected 7th to 3rd voice leading resolution.

Ex. 6.12 shows a quick ii-V-I from a solo by saxophonist Dexter Gordon.

Ex. 6.12

from a Dexter Gordon solo:

The first cell shows that a melody line can anticipate a coming chord change. Here the A note implies the F7 before it actually arrives.

The second cell uses a b9 to 5 voice leading resolution. The b9 on the F7 arrives too early to resolve directly so the resolution is delayed with a double chromatic approach from below.

Ex. 6.13 shows another fragment from a Dexter Gordon solo.

Ex. 6.13

from a Dexter Gordon solo:

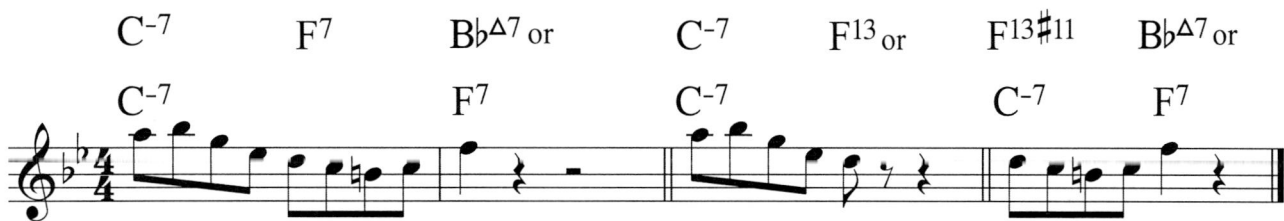

It has two possible applications; either a quick ii-V-I as in 6.12, or as the first bar of a longer two bar ii-V progression.

Some more cells extracted from bebop melodies
Now we will visit some more passages from existing bebop heads, but all transposed into the key of Bb in order to facilitate the coming re-combinations.

Ex. 6.14 shows a ii-V-I line taken from the melody of "Donna Lee."

Ex. 6.14

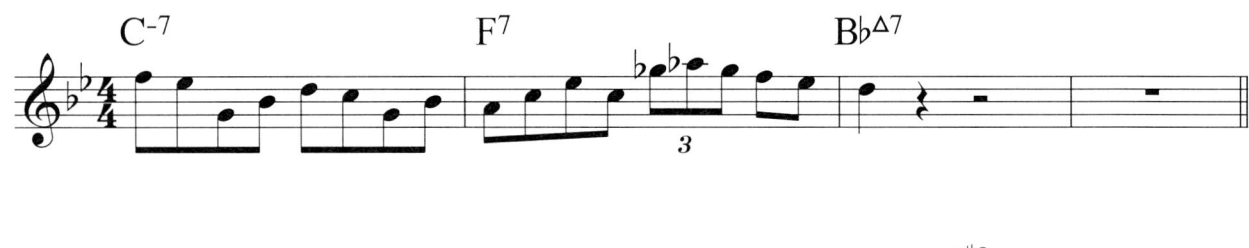

The first cell is shown isolated in bar five. Hopefully you recognize it as a re-appearance of the quote from "Honeysuckle Rose."

The second cell, isolated in bar six, uses the typical 7th to 3rd voice leading to go from the C-7 to the F7.

The third cell (bar seven) is an A diminished triad, a fragment of F7. It could have various targets, so please experiment.

The last cell (bar eight) is a common bebop lick featuring both the ♭9 and the ♯9 of the F7. Ex. 6.15 is another line taken from the melody of "Donna Lee."

Ex. 6.15

The first cell climbs chromatically, connecting the 3rd to the 5th.

The second cell is identical to the cell from 6.10 used to go from D⌀7 to G7, but fits in nicely here as well.

The third cell goes right up G7 from the 3rd to the root.

CHAPTER 6 : A DIFFERENT APPROACH TO IMPROVISING USING CELLS

The last cell is identical to the last cell from 6.14, but transposed from F7 up to G7. The final target note is E♮ since this line went to a dominant chord, but it could just as easily target E♭ if you're going to a C minor chord.

Ex. 6.16 is a ii-V-I line from the bebop classic "Move."

Ex. 6.16

from Move:

The first cell is one of those that's best with two target notes, overlapping into the next cell.

The second cell is identical to the second cell from the "Donna Lee" line in 6.14.

The third and fourth cells form a straightforward F7 line resolving into the 3rd of B♭△7.

Ex. 6.17 is a line extracted and transposed from the melody of the bridge to the bebop classic "Four Brothers."

Ex. 6.17

from Four Brothers:

The first cell is identical to the cells we've seen that connect either B♭△7 or D⌀7 to G7♭9.

The second cell is played over a B°7 in the example, but the B°7 is just a substitute for the G7♭9.

Ex. 6.18 shows a three celled fragment from the bebop tune "Dig."

Ex. 6.18

from Dig:

The first cell can be either F7, as written in the tune, or C-7.

The second cell implies C-7 going to F7, but also works fine over either chord.

The third cell targets B♮ in this melody, but there are several good alternatives available. With this target it looks identical to the cell used to connect either B♭△7 or D⌀7 to G7♭9, but in this case is used on F7 targeting the ♯11.

I took the liberty to "cheat" and include a fourth cell that was not in the original melody, but can be found in many solos by Charlie Parker and John Coltrane, among many others. Since it starts on the B♮ it can obviously follow the third cell, or even the second cell. We will find out for sure soon.

There are probably many more of these cells that can be discovered in bebop tunes and in recorded jazz solos (homework for you!), but before we continue to collect more cells, I think we should try a few re-combinations to test the idea.

Some cellular re-combinations
Let's start our cellular re-combinations with some suggested in the last example. Ex. 6.19 shows three ii-V-I lines using various re-combinations that all include the fourth cell shown in 6.18.

CHAPTER 6 : A DIFFERENT APPROACH TO IMPROVISING USING CELLS

Ex. 6.19

These lines, as well as most of the ones that follow, will be re-combinations of only cells that we have already shown and analyzed, so there will only be specific comments when further explanation may be required. One such case occurs here with the second cell in bar six. This cell was previously used only on the Bb△7 chords, while here it occurs on the F7. It is anticipating the arrival of the I chord and happens to sound great on the F7 when it is resolving to the Bb△7.

Ex. 6.20 shows a couple of re-combinations using cells from 6.13 along with some others.

Ex. 6.20

Ex. 6.21 shows re-combinations of the cells shown in 6.5 and 6.6.

Ex. 6.21

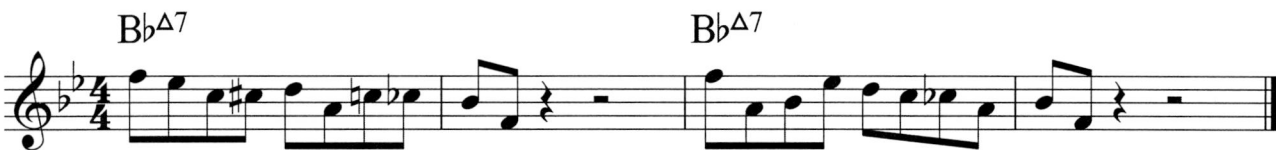

Ex. 6.22 show several re-combinations that all start with the same two cells, a combination from a Joe Pass line and a Charlie Parker line.

Ex. 6.22

The chord changes in bars 17 and 18 could be two beats each of Bb△7, E7#11 (or A7alt), Ab13#11, and G7b9. The same goes for bars 21 and 22.

CHAPTER 6 : A DIFFERENT APPROACH TO IMPROVISING USING CELLS

Ex. 6.23 shows two phrases that both start with the same combination from Joe Pass.

Ex. 6.23

The first phrase concludes with a combination from Clifford Brown while the second phrase with a combination from Charlie Parker.

Ex. 6.24 is another re-combination.

Ex. 6.24

The second cell was previously used starting on the 9th of a minor seventh chord. Here it starts on the △7th of B♭△7, which is the 9th of G-7, the relative minor of B♭.

Ex. 6.25 is a place where I've "cheated" again and included one new cell, the fourth cell in the example. You should always feel free to include and/or create new cells. Let your ear be your ultimate guide.

Ex. 6.25

Ex. 6.26 is another ii-V-I that introduces two new cells.

Ex. 6.26

The third cell is actually the "Honeysuckle Rose" quote with the order of two of the notes reversed so as to lead into the fourth cell, which is borrowed from a George Benson guitar solo.

Okay, here's one more. Ex. 6.27 is a cellular re-combination using only cells that we have already seen.

Ex. 6.27

I think that's enough re-combinations to show how the process works and to demonstrate its potential value. There are many more possible re-combinations of just the cells shown, and many more cells that can be discovered hidden in recorded jazz solos and bebop tunes, so you can have plenty to work on. Many of the possible combinations will be shown in Appendix C. Don't become overwhelmed by the large volume of material. If you work out even one re-combination and find it useful, that's one that you didn't have before, so be patient and chip away slowly over time. This will give you something to work on for years to come.

Also keep in mind that this is just one part of one aspect of jazz improvisation. It's not the one answer to everything. If you were to master hundreds of cells and thousands of re-combinations and that was all you did, you would probably be a burning bebop machine, but you would probably sound like a machine too. These cells and re-combinations can be just one item in your "bag of tricks." When you solo, always try to sing the solo through your instrument and always listen intently to what the other musicians around you are doing and you will do just fine.

APPENDIX A
HARMONIC MAJOR SCALE REVISITED

Here are some practice patterns for the harmonic major scale written in the key of C. These are shown in one octave but should be expanded as the range on your instrument allows. Of course transpose to all keys, preferably by ear and mind without writing them out.

App A ex.1 shows patterns that emphasize the use of 3rd intervals along with stepwise motion. The first four bars are the same as ex. 4.1 shown to get things started. As more consecutive 3rds are added triads and seventh chords show up.

Appendix A ex.1,

Harmonic Major Scale diatonic patterns utilizing 3rds:

APPENDIX A: *HARMONIC MAJOR SCALE REVISITED*

eight-note sequences with diatonic 7th chord arpeggios

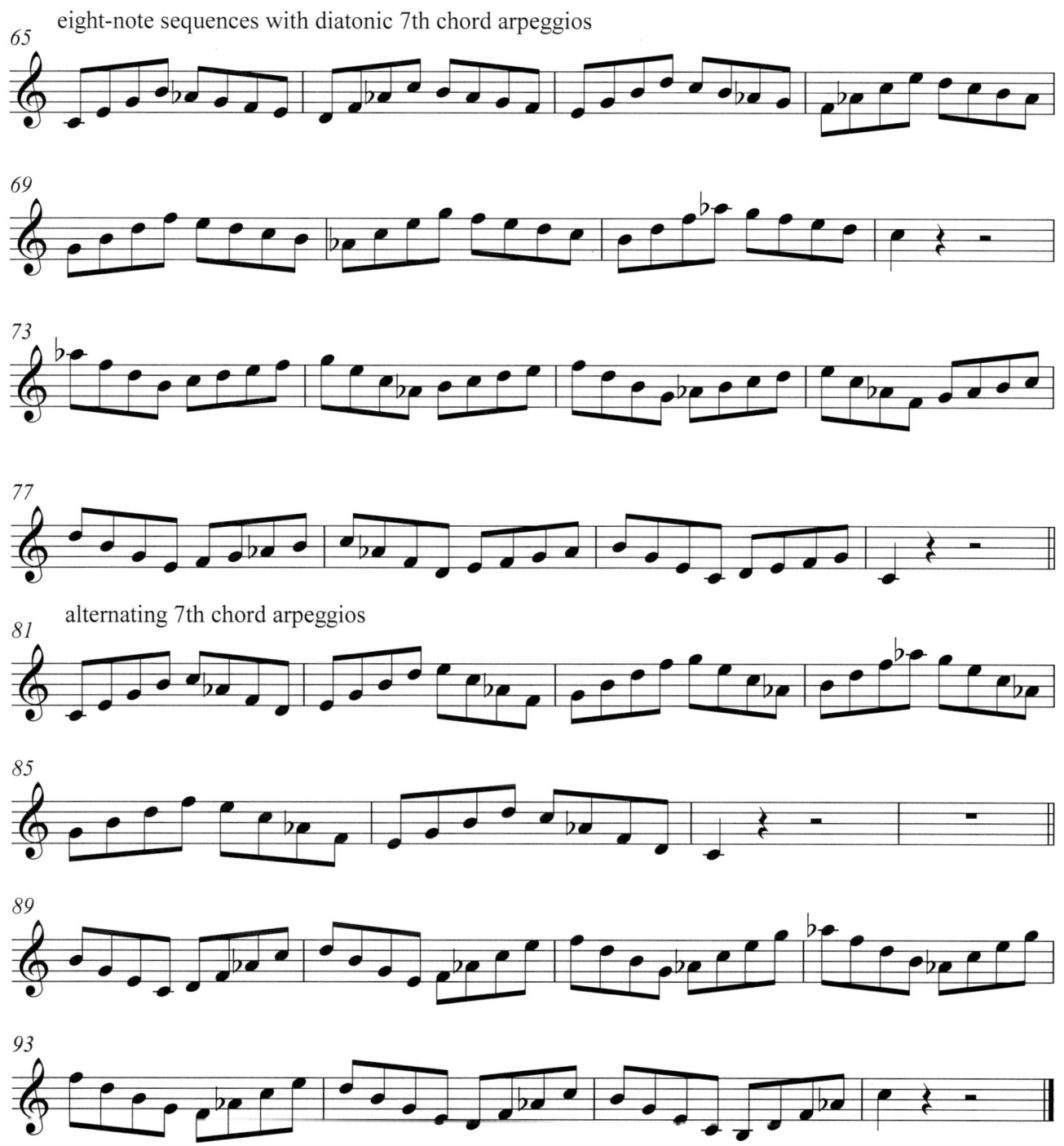

alternating 7th chord arpeggios

App A ex.2 shows some practice patterns for the harmonic major scale that use intervals wider than 3rds, along with stepwise motion and 3rds. The triads and seventh chords are connected by larger intervals in this example.

Appendix A ex.2

APPENDIX A : HARMONIC MAJOR SCALE REVISITED

33   harmonic major scale 7th chords

37

App A ex.3 shows some practice patterns for the harmonic major scale that have chromatic leading tones added. The lower neighbors are added to 3rds, triads, and seventh chords.

App A ex.3

harmonic major scale 3rds with chromatic leading tones

harmonic major scale triads with chromatic leading tones

APPENDIX A: HARMONIC MAJOR SCALE REVISITED

harmonic major scale 7th chords with chromatic leading tones

APPENDIX B
BEBOP SCALES REVISITED

Here are some studies to practice that I have found to be very helpful to facilitate my application of bebop scales to my playing. They are patterned after a typical Charlie Parker idea where he ascends an arpeggio and then descends an appropriate bebop scale or chromatic scale. These studies are designed to train the ear, mind, and fingers to find great sounding lines with harmonic relevance to the chord being played on.

App B ex.1 is based on the G dominant bebop scale. The plan is to go up an arpeggio from each of the four notes of the G7 chord, followed by a descending fragment of the bebop scale. In bar 1 the descent starts on E, which is not a chord tone of G7, so a chromatic is added to get the bebop scale back "on track." The first part of the study goes up a seventh chord before starting down, while the second part of the study goes up a ninth chord before starting down. This results in having to find different solutions depending on what note each descent starts on. The rule followed here is when there is a whole-step to the chord tone below, add the chromatic passing tone right away. When it is only a half-step to the chord tone below, add the chromatic passing tone as soon as it is appropriate to get back "on track."

APPENDIX B : BEBOP SCALES REVISITED

App B ex.1

G dominant bebop scale - ascending arpeggios with descending scales:

App B ex.2 is based on the C major bebop scale and takes the same approach as the last example. The arpeggios start from the four notes of a C6 chord. The method for solutions is the same as for the dominant bebop scale.

App B ex.2

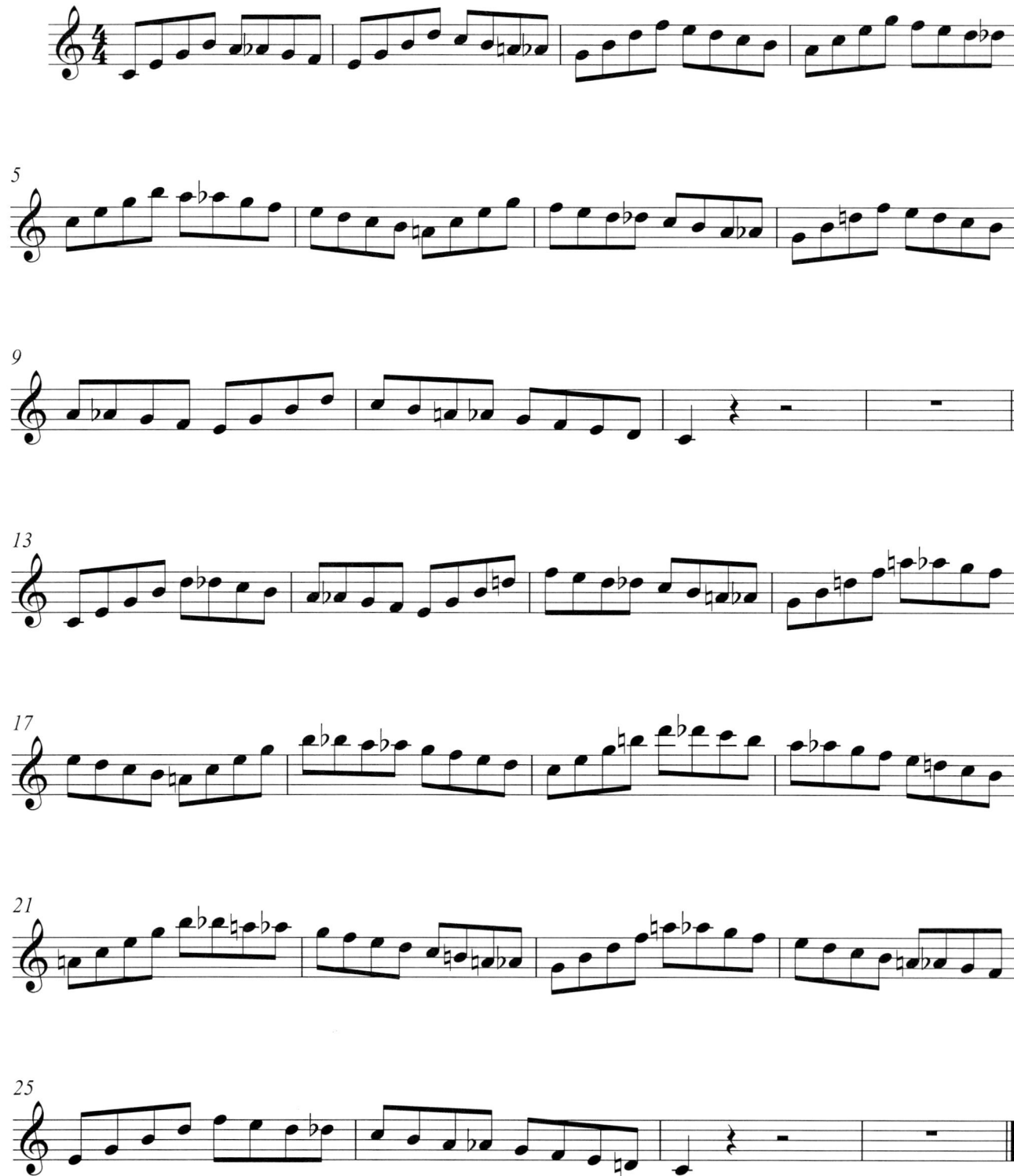

APPENDIX B : BEBOP SCALES REVISITED

App B ex.3 is based on the G dominant bebop scale with a ♭2 and a ♭6, derived from the fifth mode of the C harmonic minor scale. Since the scale has a ♭2, a ♮4, and a ♭6, they are all half-steps above the chord tones, so the method we used on the first two examples won't work here. The method used here is to form a chromatic enclosure by skipping to the half-step below the chord tone and then returning.

App B ex.3

G dominant bebop scale b2 b6 - ascending arpeggios with descending scales:

App B ex.4 is based on the C melodic minor bebop scale. It doesn't have the same problem that the last example did, so we can return the the method used for the first two examples.

App B ex.4

    C melodic minor bebop scale - ascending arpeggios with descending scales:

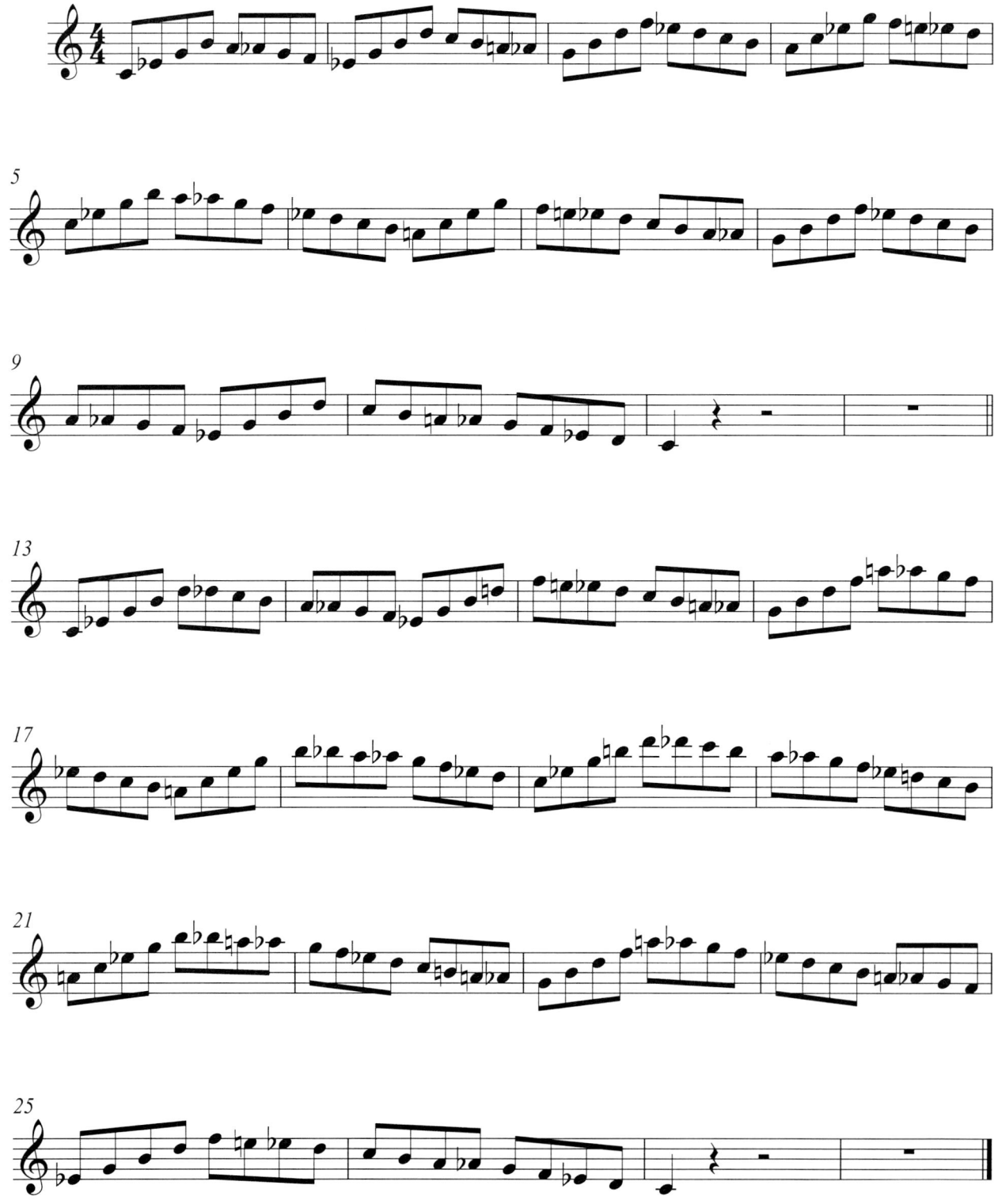

APPENDIX B: BEBOP SCALES REVISITED

The G dominant bebop scale can be used effectively not only on G7, but also on the ii-V, D-7 to G7. Then the C major bebop scale fits the I chord (C$^{\Delta 7}$), or the iii chord (E-7) or the vi chord (A-7). Likewise the G dominant ♭2 ♭6 bebop scale can be used on the minor key ii-V, D$^{\varnothing}$7 to G7, while the I chord, C-$^{\Delta 7}$ or C-6, sounds great with the C melodic minor bebop scale.

This last example ("Bebop Scales") is a summary of all the bebop scales we've looked at in detail in this book and can be looked at as a general reference or overview.

"Bebop Scales"

"Release" or Tonic Function chords (no F notes):

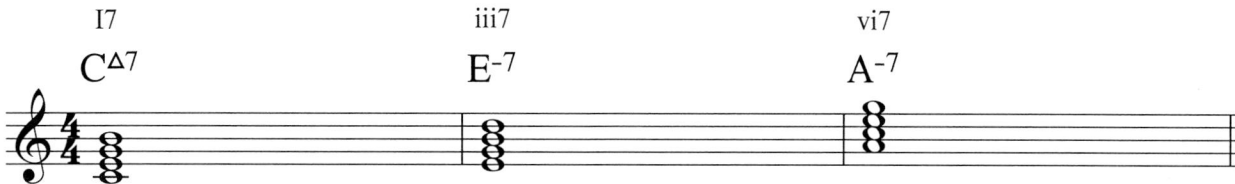

"Tension" or Dominant Function chords (all contain F notes):

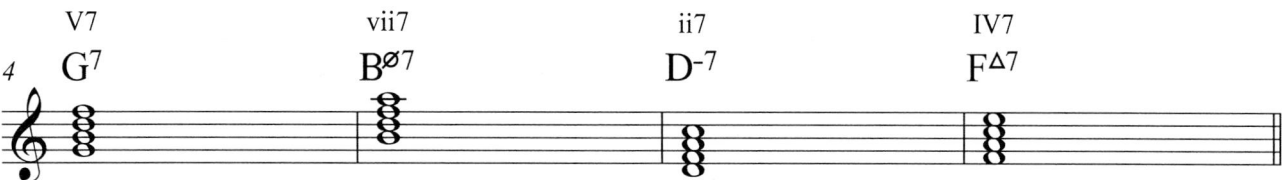

Tonic Major bebop scales fit I7, iii7, and vi7: (these keep F notes off the beat)

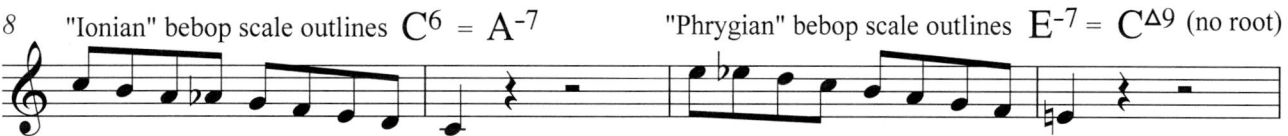

Dominant bebop scales for Major keys fit V7, vii7, ii7, and IV7:   (these place F notes on the beat)

16 "Mixolydian" bebop scale outlines G^7 "Locrian" bebop scale outlines $B^{\varnothing 7} = G^9$ (no root)

20 Ten note Dominant variation outlines $G^9 = B^{\varnothing 7}\flat 13 = D^{-13} = F^{\Delta 9 \sharp 11}$

Tonic Minor bebop scales fit all Melodic Minor chords:

23 Melodic Minor bebop scale outlines $C^{-6} = A^{\varnothing 7}$ Ten note Minor variation outlines $F^9 = C^{-6\,(add4)}$

Dominant bebop scale for minor keys fits V7 and vii°7 (and can work over ii$\varnothing$7 and iv7 and $\flat$VI$\triangle$7):

27 Dominant bebop scale for minor keys outlines G^7 but implies $G^{7\flat 13}_{\flat 9}$

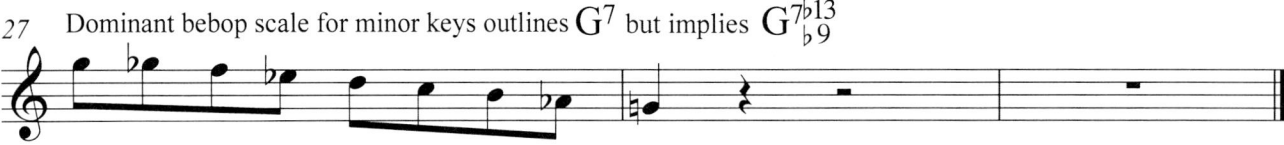

APPENDIX C
CELLULAR IMPROVISATION REVISITED

The first example shown here (Cells for combining) is a compilation I once made for myself to try as many various combinations of melodic cells for improvisation on ii-V progressions. I did it in the key of C only so it would be easier to read and transpose into all the other keys. It starts with two-beat cells, usually four notes each, that were at least 95% taken from solos on recordings, although if I remember correctly I may have contributed a very few of my own. The idea here is that the ii and the V are really part of one sound, so the lines are interchangeable for both chords. They are organized into groups based on the starting note's relationship to the chord, so the relationship to the D-7 and the relationship to the G7 are both listed for each cell, and again later for each combination. After the single cells are listed a variety of combinations are shown, again organized into groups based on the starting note's relationship to the chord. This was originally done before I fully understood the importance of the concept of each cell having one or more likely "target" notes, but I realized that they seemed important to include on the two-cell combinations. Sometimes they may appear as two notes stacked in harmony, but those are really just two different likely target notes. Sometimes the targets are two notes long, one after the other. It is entirely possible to make combinations that are three or more cells long, but I haven't done that here since this example seems long enough.

Cells for combining

APPENDIX C : CELLULAR IMPROVISATION REVISITED

RANDY VINCENT: *MAJOR IS HARMONIC*

Combinations
starting on the root of D-7 or the 5th of G7:

APPENDIX C: CELLULAR IMPROVISATION REVISITED

Combinations starting on the 3rd of D-7 or the 7th of G7:

APPENDIX C : CELLULAR IMPROVISATION REVISITED

Combinations
starting on the #4 of D-7 or the #1 of G7:

The next example (Forward Motion Cells) was done later after realizing the importance of where the cells are going, so here are many of the same cells, but now they are organized into groups of cells that share the same target notes (rather than the same starting notes). Therefore only single cells are shown (no combinations), but now the target notes are included. This way this example can be cross-referenced with the previous example to find more combinations quickly.

APPENDIX C: CELLULAR IMPROVISATION REVISITED

Forward Motion Cells

cells targeting the root of D-7 (5th of G7):

cells targeting the 9th of D-7 (13th of G7):

APPENDIX C : CELLULAR IMPROVISATION REVISITED

cells targeting the maj7th of D-7 (#11th of G7):

APPENDIX C : CELLULAR IMPROVISATION REVISITED

App C ex.3 demonstrates how this process might work.

App C ex.3

Forward motion cell bar 1
combined with Cells for combining bar 1:

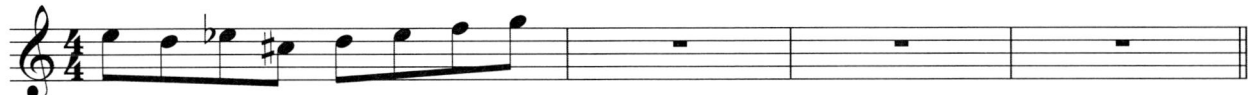

Forward motion cell bar1
combined with Cells for combining bar 75:

Forward motion cell bar1
combined with Cells for combining bar 101:

Forward motion cell bar 20
combined with Cells for combining bar 145:

A longer combination using a variety of cells
found in Cells for combining and in Forward motion cells:

The top line simply attaches the first bar of "Cells for combining" (starting on the root of D-7 or the 5th of G7), but up an octave, to the first bar of "Forward Motion Cells" (targeting root of D-7 or the 5th of G7) to demonstrate how they flow together.

The next line (starting at bar 5) starts the same but uses the combination shown in bar 75 of "Cells for combining."

The next line (starting at bar 9) also uses the first bar of "Forward Motion Cells" but continues with the combination shown in bar 101 of "Cells for combining."

For the next line (starting at bar13) I thought I would try a random combination from a completely different place to see what would happen. This time the first line is from bar 20 of "Forward Motion Cells," targeting the 9th of D-7 or the 13th of G7, and then continuing with the combination shown in bar 145 of "Cells for combining." To my ear the result flows nicely and has all the melodic qualities of good bebop jazz, even though I've never heard that exact line before. I think this demonstrates how using the vocabulary of jazz can be used to create your own convincing lines for soloing.

The last line (starting at bar17) shows a sample longer line using the same process, and only (of course) cells shown in "Forward Motion Cells" and in "Cells for combining."

Not every combination that I have tried always produced results that I was happy with, so I don't waste any time transposing and practicing those. However, there are literally thousands of possible good combinations that can be found. I know this may seem like a lot, but keep in mind that you can "test drive" a bunch of combinations and then pick some of your favorites to memorize and practice in all keys. I certainly haven't mastered them all (far from it), but they are here for your continued use for hopefully many years to come.

APPENDIX D:
SOME INTERESTING WAYS TO THINK ABOUT SCALES

These next examples show some interesting ways to think about scales. For quite some time now I have thought of scales as not just collections of pitches, but rather as collections of chords that work in a certain way together to create a sense of what we call "tonality." The first example I'm going to show was inspired by the amazing book *Harmonic Experience* by W. A. Mathieu. It contained "harmonic maps" of the many varied scales and modes that gave me some deeper insight into how they worked to create their "magic." "Scales as Triads" demonstrates.

Scales as Triads

F Lydian = C major scale:

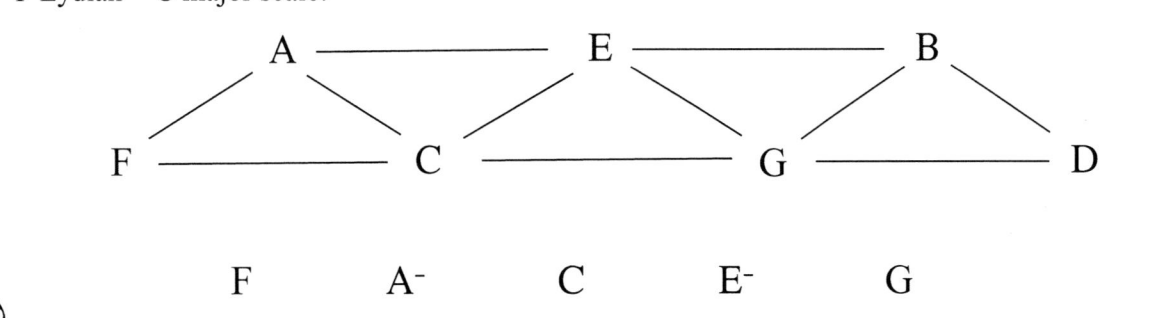

F Dorian = C natural minor scale:

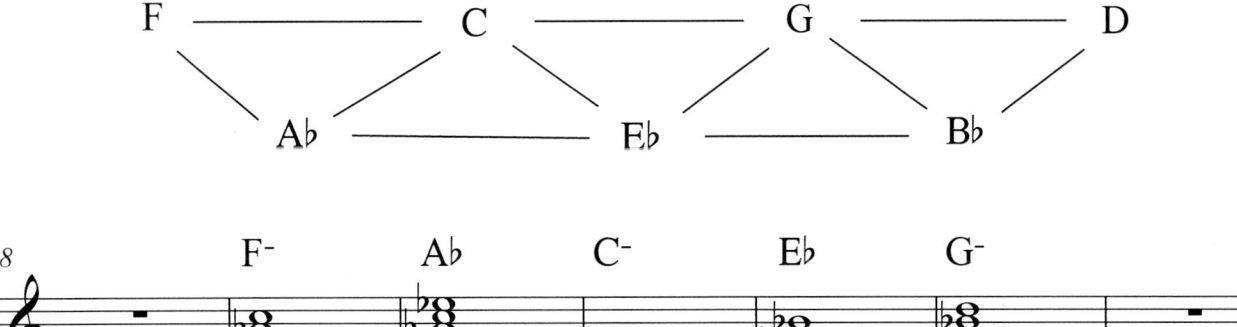

F Lydian Dominant = C melodic minor scale:

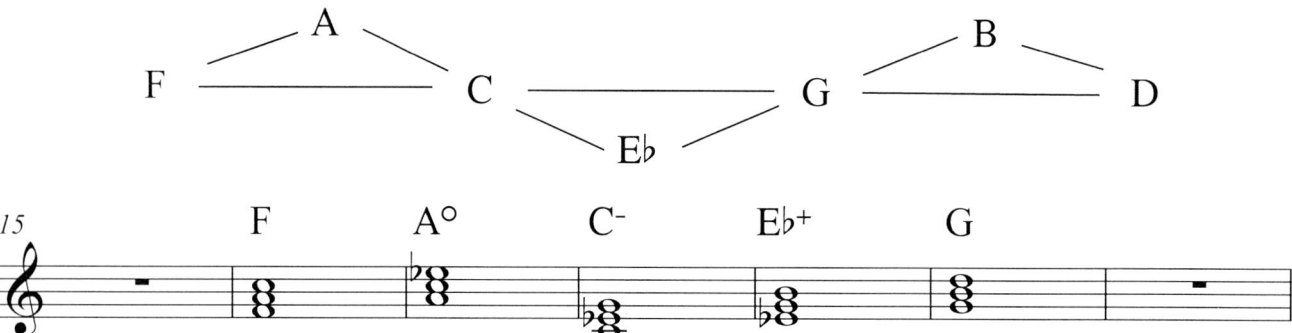

F Lydian Minor = C harmonic major scale:

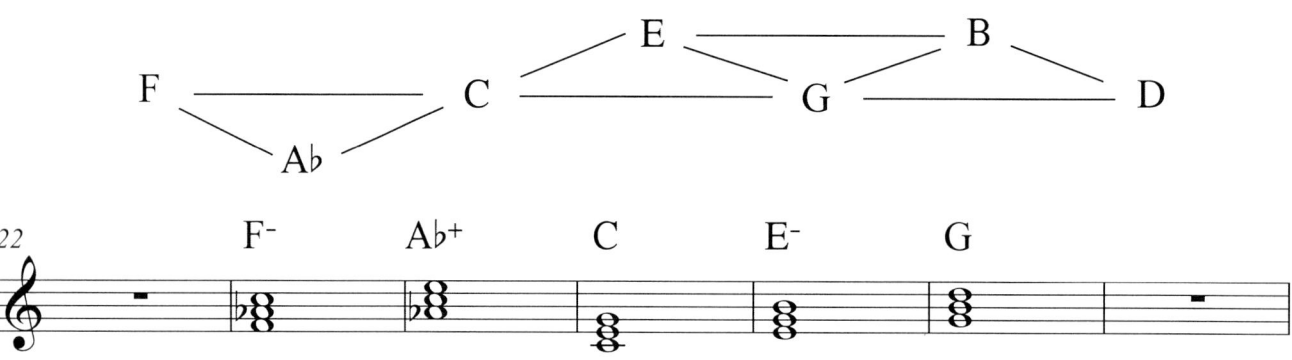

F Dorian #4 = C harmonic minor scale:

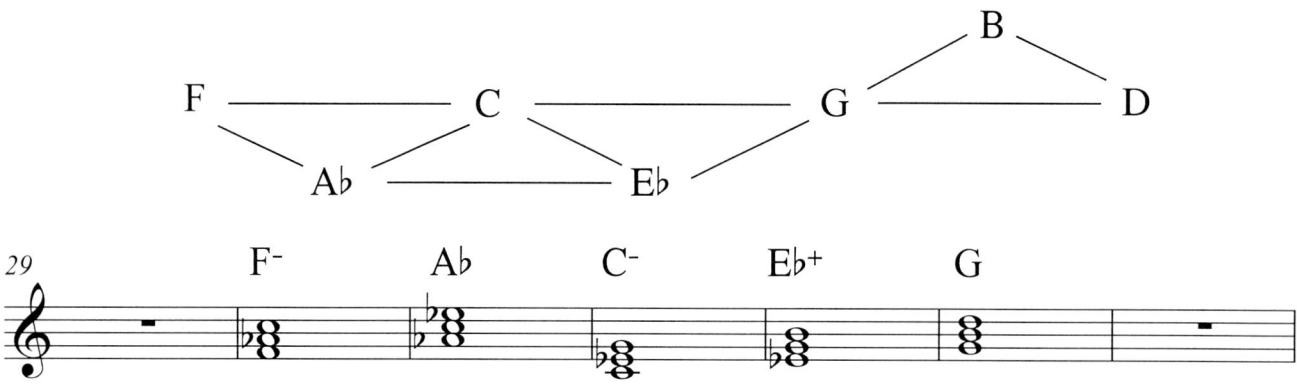

APPENDIX D : *SOME INTERESTING WAYS TO THINK ABOUT SCALES*

F Melodic Minor scale = C "Backdoor" scale:

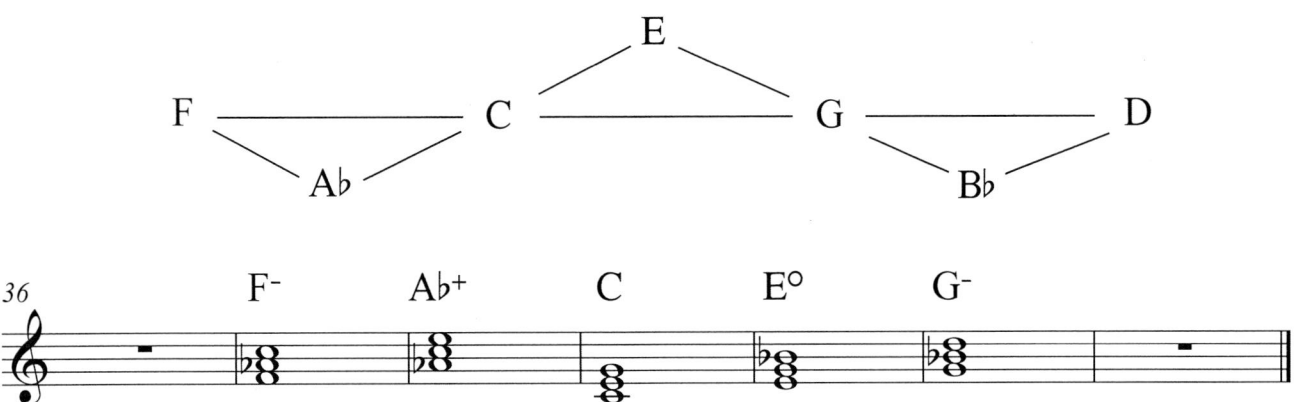

The concept is the idea that a tonic has a "dominant," the 5th above, and a "sub-dominant," the 5th below, and that a major triad or a minor triad can be built on each of those steps to create a scale. This means that the dominant has a perfect 5th above it as well. So the way I've decided to draw my own version of the harmonic maps is to lay the notes out so that any perfect 5th is represented by a horizontal line with the lower note of the 5th to the left and the upper note of the 5th to the right. A major 3rd interval is represented by a diagonal line with the lower note to the lower left and the upper note to the upper right. And consequently a minor 3rd interval is represented by a diagonal line with the lower note to the upper left and the higher note to the lower right. So triads are represented by triangles. The major triad triangles point up, while the minor triad triangles point down.

In this first example we see same spine of 5ths in each type of scale. We read left to right, so first a name is given for each "F" mode. But being the sub-dominant means that the main scale for each tonality is named from the C tonic. Therefore the first scale shown is F lydian mode but is actually the C major scale. And similarly for the other scales shown.

For the major scale and the natural minor scale all of the triads are represented by triangles and form an interlocking pattern of alternating major and minor triads. For the other scales there are other triad types as well. Two diagonal lines crossing the central spine and angling up from left to right form an augmented triad (two consecutive major 3rds), while two diagonal lines crossing the central spine and angling down from left to right form a diminished triad (two consecutive minor 3rds). In all of the scales the F triads, the C triads, and the G triads are all always either major triads or minor triads.

You might be wondering what the heck is a C "Backdoor" scale. All of the other scales in the example have been covered already. The Backdoor scale gets its name from the fact that it can generate what jazz musicians call the "backdoor dominant," a dominant seventh chord built on the ♭7 of a major key and can resolve directly back to the tonic major chord. It frequently happens over a pedal bass on the tonic or on the dominant. Examples include "A Child Is Born" by Thad Jones and "The Summer Knows" by Michel Legrand. The B♭7 could be disguised as F-6 or D⌀7 among other possibilities, and can have a ♮9th, a ♯11th, and a ♮13th. Some other names for this scale include B♭ lydian dominant, C mixolydian ♭6 and C natural minor over C major. I can also hear it as C aeolian mode with a major 3rd.

This final example shows these scales (plus one) as two chord cadences.

App D ex.2

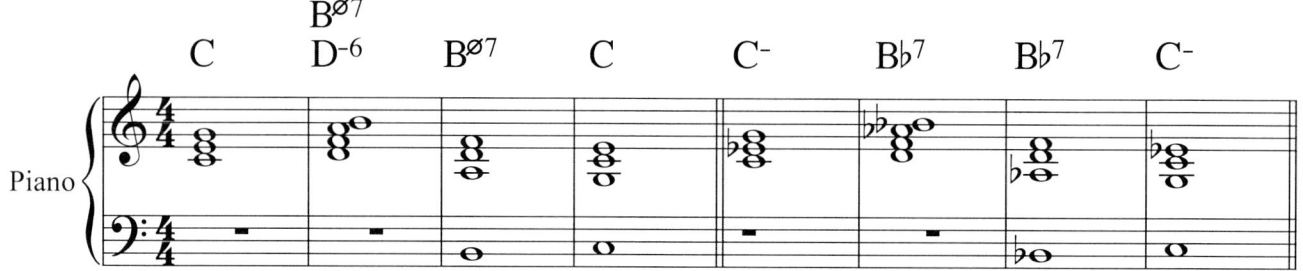

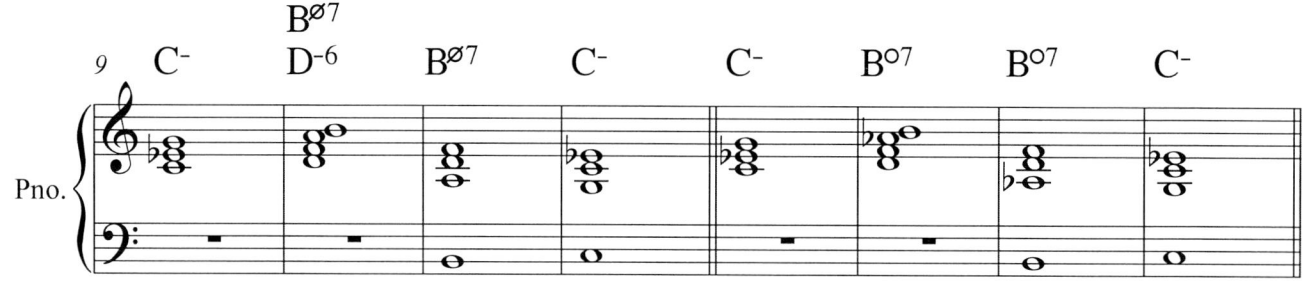

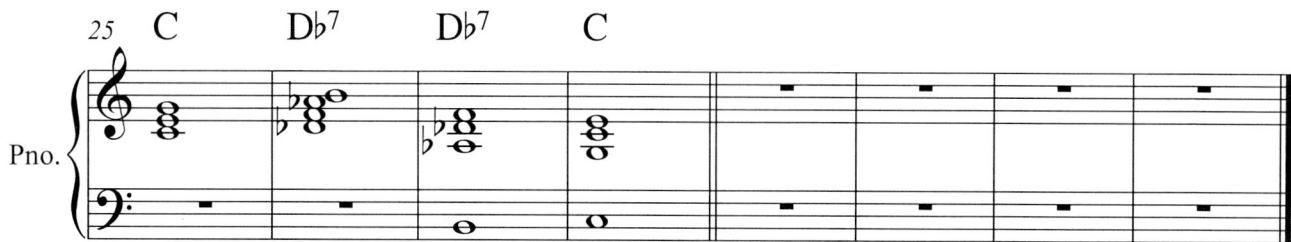

APPENDIX D : SOME INTERESTING WAYS TO THINK ABOUT SCALES

The idea is to suggest that the tonic C major triad or C minor triad from the previous chart is the only fully consonant resolution in the tonality, so a chord made of all the other notes from the scale will create a penultimate cadential chord that defines the rest of each tonality. At first the tonic triad is shown, followed by the other notes in scale order and given a name (or two). Then the penultimate chord is shown in a piano voicing resolving to the tonic and using contrary motion between the top voice and the bottom voice. The double harmonic scale (aka "Byzantine" scale) forms what jazz musicians usually think of as a tritone substitute dominant seventh chord (♭II for V), or D♭7 for G7 in this case. The spelling of D♭ to B♮ here suggests what classical theorists call an "augmented 6th" chord.

Okay, just one more example for guitar players. It is the same two chord cadences example but written for guitar and showing chord diagrams for the cadences.

Scales as Two Chord Cadences

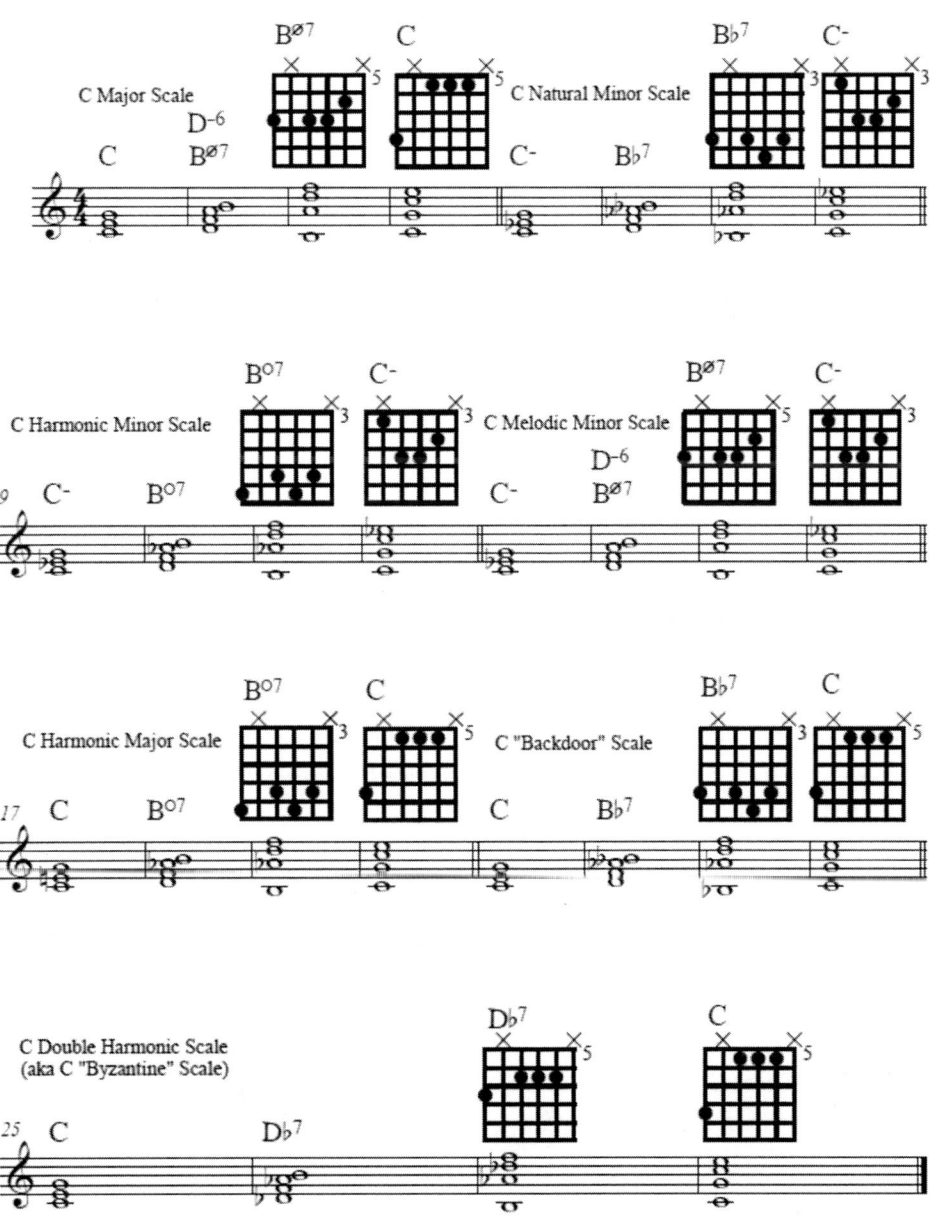

The Sher Music Co. Catalog

BEST-SELLING BOOKS BY MARK LEVINE
The Jazz Theory Book
The Jazz Piano Book
Jazz Piano Masterclass: The Drop 2 Book
How To Voice Standards at the Piano

THE WORLD'S BEST FAKE BOOKS
The New Real Book - Vol. 1 - C, Bb and Eb
The New Real Book - Vol. 2 - C, Bb and Eb
The New Real Book - Vol. 3 - C, Bb, Eb & Bass Clef

The Real Easy Book - Vol. 1 - C, Bb, Eb & Bass Clef
The Real Easy Book - Vol. 2 - C, Bb, Eb & Bass Clef
The Real Easy Book - Vol. 3 - C, Bb, Eb & Bass Clef
The Latin Real Easy Book - C, Bb, Eb & Bass Clef
Drum Supplement for Real Easy Book - Vol. 1

The Standards Real Book - C, Bb and Eb
The Latin Real Book - C, Bb and Eb
The Real Cool Book - Octet charts from the 1950s
The All-Jazz Real Book - with selected audio
The European Real Book - with selected audio
The Best of Sher Music Real Books - C, Bb & Eb
The World's Greatest Fake Book - C only
Jazz Arrangements of Public Domain Songs
The Yellowjackets Songbook - separate parts

LATIN MUSIC BOOKS
Contemporary Latin Jazz Guitar - by Neff Irizarry
Decoding Afro-Cuban Jazz - by Mauleon & Valdes
The Salsa Guidebook - by Rebeca Mauleõn
101 Montunos - by Rebeca Mauleõn
The Latin Bass Book - by Oscar Stagnaro & Chuck Sher
The Latin Real Book - C, Bb, & Eb
The True Cuban Bass - by Carlos del Puerto
The Brazilian Guitar Book - by Nelson Faria
Inside the Brazilian Rhythm Section - Faria/Korman
Conga Drummer's Guidebook - by Michael Spiro
Language of the Masters - by Michael Spiro
Introduction to the Conga Drum DVD - by M. Spiro
Afro-Caribbean Grooves for Drumset - JPhi Fanfant
Afro-Peruvian Percussion Ensemble - H. Morales
Flamenco Improvisation - Vol.1-3 by Enrique Vargas
Muy Caliente! - Afro-Cuban Book & Play-Aong audio
Music of the Arará Savalú Cabildo - Galvin & Spiro

DIGITAL FAKE BOOKS
The New Real Book - Vol.1 - C, Bb & Eb
The Digital Standards Songbook - individual songs with lyrics, plus C, Bb, Eb, High Voice & Low Voice
The Digital Real Book (650 songs from all our books)

THE DIGITAL SONGBOOK SERIES
The Kenny Barron Songbook
The Carla Bley Songbook
The Tom Harrell Songbook
The Oscar Hernandez Songbook
The Alan Pasqua Songbook
The Horace Silver Songbook
The Steve Swallow Songbook
The Ralph Towner Songbook
The Wayne Wallace Songbook
The Kenner Werner Songbook
The Randy Brecker Songbook
The Larry Dunlap Songbook
The Barry Finnerty Songbook
The Benny Golson Songbook
The Steve Khan Songbook
The Doug Morton Songbook
The Andy Narell Songbook
The Enrico Pieranunzi Songbook
The Dave Tull Songbook
The Denny Zeitlin Songbook

FOR STUDENT MUSICIANS
The Real Easy Book - Vol. 1 - C, Bb, Eb & Bass Clef
The Real Easy Book - Vol. 2 - C, Bb, Eb & Bass Clef
The Real Easy Book - Vol. 3 - C, Bb, Eb & Bass Clef
The Latin Real Easy Book - C, Bb, Eb & Bass Clef
Drum Supplement for Real Easy Book - Vol. 1
The Blues Scales - C, Bb, Eb, Bass Clef & Guitar
Rhythm First! - C, Bb, Eb & Bass Clef - by Tom Kamp
Guitarist's Introduction to Jazz - by Randy Vincent
Walking Bassics - by Ed Fuqua
Foundation Exercises for Bass - by Chuck Sher

CDs
Poetry+Jazz: A Magical Marriage - by Chuck Sher
Play-Along CDs for The New Real Book - Vol.1
The Latin Real Book Sampler CD

continued on next page

SHER MUSIC CO. JAZZ METHOD BOOKS
available in both print & digital forms

GUITAR
Jazz Guitar Voicings: The Drop 2 Book
   - Randy Vincent
Three-Note Voicings and Beyond - Randy Vincent
Line Games - Randy Vincent
Jazz Guitar Soloing: The Cellular Approach
   - Randy Vincent
The Guitarist's Introduction to Jazz - Randy Vincent
Contemporary Latin Jazz Guitar - Neff Irizarry

PIANO
The Jazz Piano Book - Mark Levine
Jazz Piano Masterclass: The Drop 2 Book - M. Levine
How To Voice Standards at the Piano - Mark Levine
An Approach to Comping - Vol. 1 - Jeb Patton
An Approach to Comping - Vol. 2 - Jeb Patton
Introduction to Jazz Piano: A Deep Dive - Jeb Patton
Playing for Singers - Mike Greensill
Wisdom of the Hand - Marius Nordal
The Jazz Solos of Chick Corea - Peter Sprague

SAXOPHONE
The Practice Notebooks of Michael Brecker
The Jazz Saxophone Book - Tim Armacost
Logic and Critical Thinking in Jazz Improvisation
   - Vincent Herring

VOICE
The Digital Standards Songbook - individual songs
   with lyrics, plus C, Bb, Eb, High Voice & Low Voice
The Jazz Singer's Guidebook - David Berkman

DRUMS
Syncopation Companion - Bryan Bowman
Inner Drumming - George Marsh
Drum Supplement for Real Easy Book Vol.1 - Alan Hall
Afro-Caribbean Grooves for Drumset - JPhi Fanfant

TRUMPET
New Orleans Trumpet - Jim Thornton
Modern Etudes for Solo Trumpet - Cameron Pearce

BASS
The Improvisor's Bass Method - Chuck Sher
Concepts for Bass Soloing - Marc Johnson & C. Sher
Walking Bassics - Ed Fuqua
Foundation Exercises for Bass - Chuck Sher
Walking Bass Line Construction - F Blues - Bob Sinicrope

JAZZ THEORY AND HARMONY
The Jazz Theory Book - Mark Levine
The Jazz Harmony Book - David Berkman
Forward Motion - Hal Galper
Metaphors for the Musician - Randy Halberstadt
Minor is Major! - Dan Greenblatt
Rhythm Changes Guide - Lukas Gabric
Jazz Scores and Analysis - Vol.1 - Richard Lawn
Jazz Scores and Analysis - Vol. 2 - Richard Lawn
The Blues Scales - C, Bb, Eb, Bass Clef & Guitar
   - Dan Greenblatt
Logic and Critical Thinking in Jazz Improvisation
   - Vincent Herring

PRACTICE GUIDES
The Practice Notebooks of Michael Brecker
Jazz Musician's Guide to Creative Practicing
   - David Berkman
The Serious Jazz Practice Book - Barry Finnerty
The Serious Jazz Book II - Barry Finnerty
Building Solo Lines from Cells - Randy Vincent
365 Days of Practice - Rick Margitza
The Bob Mover Jazz Lexicon - Bob Mover

EAR TRAINING
The Real Easy Ear Training Book - Roberta Radley
Reading, Writing and Rhythmetic - Roberta Radley

RHYTHM SECTION GUIDES
Essential Grooves - Moretti, Stagnaro & Nicholl
Inside the Brazilian Rhythm Section - Nelson Faria
   & Cliff Korman
The Salsa Guidebook - Rebeca Mauleõn
Decoding Afro-Cuban Jazz - Mauleõn & Valdes

BILINGUAL OR LIBROS EN ESPANOL
101 Montunos - Rebeca Mauleõn
Muy Caliente! - Afro-Cuban Book & Play-Along
El Libro del Jazz Piano - Mark Levine
The Latin Real Book - C, Bb and Eb

MISCELLANEOUS
Method for Chromatic Harmonica - Max de Aloe
Jazz Songs for the Student Violinist
   - Kevin Mitchell & Joanne Keefe

*Sign up for our monthly discount newsletter
by writing shermuse@sonic.net*